112421

One Twelve Four Twenty One

Tanya A Dodge

WestBow®
PRESS
A DIVISION OF THOMAS NELSON
& ZONDERVAN

Scripture taken from the New King James Version. Copyright © 1979, 1980, 1982 by Thomas Nelson, Inc. Used by permission. All rights reserved.

WestBow Press books may be ordered through booksellers or by contacting:

WestBow Press
A Division of Thomas Nelson & Zondervan
1663 Liberty Drive
Bloomington, IN 47403
www.westbowpress.com
1 (866) 928-1240

ISBN: 978-1-4908-6842-4 (sc)
ISBN: 978-1-4908-6843-1 (hc)
ISBN: 978-1-4908-6841-7 (e)

Library of Congress Control Number: 2015901580

Print information available on the last page.

WestBow Press rev. date: 03/25/2015

Dedication

To all those who are struggling to find
joy and purpose in their lives.

:

Contents

Section Two
How it All Changed: A New Creation

Section Three
New Things Have Come

Foreword

When he walked in the doors of our church, to say that it was obvious that Doug had a story would be the understatement of the year. Oddly, it wasn't the tattoos that made his arms look like a wall covered in graffiti that made him stick out, it was the obvious demeanor of a man who was at peace: peace with God, peace with his wife, and peace with himself.

Doug is a big man! I shook his hand and the grip almost turned into an arm wrestling match as if we were trying to find out who could out love the other with a firm handshake. He grabbed my hand as if to say, "I want to know you and I want to tell you my story."

We were instant friends!

His story came to me in bits and pieces. After all, there is a lot to digest. You might even call his story intimidating. As the story began to pour out, the thought occurred to me, "Wow! Everyone needs to hear this!" So, I said, "Dude, you have to write a book." It wasn't the first time he had heard that.

I am writing this forward to plead with you to read Doug's story. The first half reads like the script of a TV show where a man, a victim of a bad home life, bad decisions, bad relationships, and bad substance abuse finds himself in a cold cement room.

It is riveting because we can relate to so much of Doug's story about the pain of life and the terrible consequences of poor choices. On the other hand, so much of Doug's story is so extreme, we can't possibly imagine how it must have felt.

Truth is, though the first half is riveting, it is not the most interesting! The second half is the miracle. The story turns from being about Doug to being about a God who loved Doug with no strings attached, and I mean **no strings**. If there was anyone that God had reason not to love or forgive, Doug would be a good candidate.

Doug, however, came face to face with someone who would never reject him, never harm him, and never run from him. Instead, God loved him, forgave him, and completely changed him…and by change, I mean made him a radical new man! To look at Doug you see the evidence of the old life. He still is a biker, rides a Street Glide to be exact. He still wears a black leather vest and is still as strong as an ox. On the inside, though, Doug is a new creation.

And that is the story!

If you wonder if God is real or if you are worthy of God's love, you don't have to go any further than Doug Dodge to find a trophy of God's love and grace!

I am proud to call Doug my friend, honored to be an honorary member of Forged by Fire, and blessed to be called Doug's pastor.

I will warn you, if you start to read this story, you won't be able to put it down. It is a best seller, a best seller about Jesus and how far He will go to chase you down.

Dr. David Smith
Lead Pastor, Fairhaven Church
Centerville, Ohio

Preface

From the author: Judging by appearances alone, Doug and I seem to be an unlikely couple. In some ways, we are an unlikely couple. He is tall and beefy. I am petite. He is covered with tattoos, the kind people got before it was a fashion statement. I have no tattoos. He is loud. I am quiet. You get the idea.

Add God to the equation and it all makes sense. Someone once said to me, "When I first saw you two I wouldn't have expected you to be a couple, but when I heard Doug speak I knew why." Though Doug and I are almost perfect opposites, we both love the Lord. God is the glue that binds us, and together we are able to touch the lives of many more people than either of us could by ourselves.

One of Doug's favorite ways to share the hope of Christ is to engage people in conversation. I mean **anywhere** and with **anybody**. Once, we were eating dinner at a local diner and he started one of these conversations with a man at a neighboring table. Doug ended up leading that man in the Sinner's Prayer right there in the middle of the restaurant! I joked that people were going to start calling Doug the restaurant evangelist. He's not afraid to talk about Jesus no matter where he is.

Doug is often invited to share his story at churches and schools, and he never turns them down. I was initially inspired to write this book after seeing countless people deeply touched by hearing Doug's story. I have seen hope borne in both those who are trying to help someone as well as those who are hurting.

We have all seen stories on the news, or known someone personally, who caused us to wonder, "What makes someone become...(fill in the blank-violent, an addict-the malady doesn't matter)?" Doug's story highlights that we all start out the same, as sweet, innocent babies, but things like the type of family we happen to be born into, a lack of resources, witnessing violence, drug abuse, and sexual abuse impact the type of life we lead.

Doug's story could be the story of any one of us. All we can do is thank God if we have grown up in a household where we didn't have to worry if the lights were going to stay on, if we would have clean clothes to wear to school, or who was going to get beaten that night. May this book ignite compassion within those who have more resources than they need, and give hope to those who don't have enough.

Acknowledgement

We hereby acknowledge the following people and organizations for their contributions to this book: This book would not be possible without the support of our children, who inspire us to be our best. We thank the pastors who have led us in the past, and those who continue to guide us today. Thanks to the teachers at the Academy, Kim and Becky, and their students for encouraging Doug to share his story in print. Thank you to MaryBeth and Debbie for helping us stay sane. We thank each other for the patience and stamina it took to create this book. Thank you to Laura for editing. We appreciate Seth and Brent for their commitment to this project. We couldn't have done this without friends like Lisa K. and Amy B. who give so freely of themselves; not only to us but to the children they serve. Thank you to the teachers who inspire us to love reading and writing.

Special thanks from Doug to Don and Wanda for the prayers that started it all. Thanks from Tanya to Mom and Dad for making sure I was read to every night as a child. Last but not least, thank you to Westbow Press for your help with the final production of this book.

Prologue

Decisions, Decisions...

I could feel the familiar weight of the 9mm Beretta laying up against my heart in the breast pocket of my jacket. I had stopped unannounced at Greg's old farmhouse in the country that night. When he came to the door, I sensed that he didn't want me there. I found out why after he let me in. A package containing what looked to be about $100,000 worth of Chrystal meth had just arrived in the mail. Greg told me to hang out in the kitchen while he took care of something in the other room. While sitting there, a thought came to me: "What could I do with Greg's body?" No one knew I was there. How easy would it be to put a bullet in him and take all the dope for myself? This is what my life had come to. The decisions I was making were not where to send my kids to college or where to go on vacation, but how I would dispose of a body and get away with murder.

SECTION ONE

How it All Started

CHAPTER 1

Let's Start at the Beginning

Of course, I didn't start out this way. I was born in Sarasota, Florida in 1961. I remember growing up around all the things the Gulf Coast had to offer. Beautiful sun-drenched days, ivory white sand, and the ocean. With all that great weather, we weren't inside much. My younger brother and sister and I explored the marinas and canals every chance we got. I would look at the different types of boats and imagine what great adventures the people on them were going to or coming from. When you don't have much, you learn how to make your own fun. Something as simple as a stick could be a gun, a horse, or a lot of different things. We lived across the street from an orange grove and spent hours just lying in the tops of those trees, eating the fresh fruit that came from them, and talking about all the wonderful things we were going to do when we grew up. Had I known what was to come, I would never have come down from that tree.

But for now, I was just a child who liked being outside. My dad worked as the custodian of a department store in Sarasota for twelve years. My mom stayed at home to take care of us kids. We had lots of animals. Right at our house we had ducks, chickens, rabbits, goats, and a spider monkey called Penny. We had some hogs that we kept at Miss Stevens' house, where my mom and dad rented some pasture. My dad once traded her a 750 pound boar hog for a shotgun, which I still have today. My brother and I rode horses, goats...we'd ride anything. We had fun outside. Everything was good outside. Things were different inside. As it turned out, future events in my life would only serve to reinforce this idea: outside was good; inside was bad.

As a child, I liked to be outside and away from everybody but my brother and sister. I thought it was because there wasn't anything to do inside, but now that I think about it, I realize it was because I didn't like the things that were going on inside the house. Both my mom and dad were pretty heavy drinkers. When dad wasn't at work, he was usually drinking with my mom. We didn't have a whole lot of money, so we wore the same clothes a lot. Children can be pretty brutal about things like that. I hated school. But more about that later…

I *did* like going to Sunday school. One of the fondest memories I have is of the church bus pulling up outside the house and me running across the yard to get on. Everybody treated you nicely. They talked about something called *Scriptures,* and I learned about this guy named Jesus. He would never hurt me, and I could trust Him. We sang songs about Jesus. I remember a picture on the wall of this man Jesus with a group of small children. When I looked at it, I'd think about how I wanted to be one of the children in the picture. The church bus was like leaving one part of my life behind. Just as soon as they opened that door, I ran in. I was leaving my life behind and, for a while, I could forget about it. I really liked riding the church bus. This was my life until I was 11 years old when everything changed.

Things felt a lot different indoors. I felt trapped. That's where my dad got violent. He liked to hit my mom. I shouldn't say he liked to, but he definitely did it. He probably regretted it later. I just have to say it: my dad was a mean drunk. If there really is something called "short-man syndrome," he had it, and the alcohol only made it worse. He was less than five foot three inches tall. In fact, my whole family was short. My mom was five one and my sister topped out at five two. By the time I was done growing, I was six one. I think my dad held that against me.

When he was drinking, he was quick to go off on my brother and me for any little thing that we would do. He'd get the belt out and make us lay down on the bed. He made us lay there while he whipped us with the belt. Sometimes my mom would intervene and talk him into letting her *take* the whipping. Sometimes my mother would talk him into letting her *give* the whipping. At the time, I think I hated her for that, but as I grew older I understood that she did that to save us from the hard beating from my dad. She was saving us from something worse.

It was a really bad situation indoors. I remember my dad getting drunk one time and smacking my mom, my brother, and me yet again. He never touched my sister, and I was really thankful for that, but I was also sick and tired of us getting knocked around. I was only nine or ten years old, but I was already forming an attitude that stayed with me for a long time: "You might be able to beat me, but you can't break me." I hoped that one day, the tables would be turned, and he wouldn't have the upper hand anymore.

Until the day I could match him physically, the only way I knew to hurt him back was to break something that I knew he loved. As soon as my dad passed out that night, I broke one of his favorite toys, a prized pistol called a Ruger Blackhawk. That night, when everybody was passed out, I took that pistol out and beat it on the rails of the railroad track that ran behind our house. I beat the handle off of it. I bent the barrel. At my young age, I was already full of rage. I gathered up all the pieces and took them back in the house, even though I knew the consequences were going to hurt. In my mind then, and for many years to come, there were some things worth doing despite painful consequences.

The next morning, things were hot around the Dodge household! I don't know if my mom intervened, but I'd like to think that just once she explained to my dad that the situation must be pretty bad for me do something like that even though I knew the consequences. I never got touched for that. I remember that my dad took that gun and sent it in the mail to get it worked on. He almost got put in jail for that. He didn't know you weren't allowed to send guns through the mail.

Things continued like that until I was eleven years old: My dad going to work, coming home, and drinking. My parents not only fought with each other, they also fought with other couples they drank with. Other couples would come over; they'd get in a fight; and within a month, they'd be back drinking together again. I remember one night my dad's best friend, I believe his name was Mark, and his wife were over drinking. The moms and kids were in the living room. Mark and dad were in the kitchen. All at once we heard a loud bang, and when we ran into the kitchen, we saw Mark on the floor. He was bleeding from the head. My dad had been showing him a set of what he thought were unloaded Derringers. They were always showing each other their guns, going out to the creek and shooting them. Well, it turns out that my dad was not living under the old adage "Always treat a gun as if it's loaded." My dad discovered, once he pulled the trigger, that there was a bullet in it. Luckily, it just grazed Mark's head. Mark was dazed for a minute, but when he woke up a little, they bandaged it up. Witnessing this type of scene was normal to me.

CHAPTER 2

From a Shotgun to a Swingblade

My eleventh year of life is when everything seemed to come to a climax. My parents had been drinking with the neighbors, a couple that lived there and some brothers of either the husband or the wife, and they got into the fight. I remember my mom getting punched in the face by one of the men, and my dad fighting them. The police come out, broke up the fight, and told everyone to go home. Then, the police officer pulled around to the front corner of the church parking lot across the street to do paperwork on the incident. Suddenly, there was an explosion out in front of my house. It sounded like a loud pop. Those same men from the fight earlier were back! My dad grabbed me, yelling, "Here's how you take care of this!" He took a gun out of the closet, pushed the screen door open with his foot and, with the gun down around hip level, shot one of the men who was in the front yard. He went down in the ditch and the other men ran off. I noticed the sound of the screen door slamming shut as my dad moved to come back in. I thought about how mom yelled at us kids for letting the screen door slam. My dad had just shot a man and my focus was on the slam of the screen door. That just shows you that my reference point was screwed up. Chaos was so normal to me that a man could be shot in front of me, and I was thinking about Mom yelling at us for letting the door slam shut.

The next thing I knew, the house was full of police and they were dragging my dad out. We found out later that the porch light had blown, but, in that moment, what my parents heard was a gunshot and Dad reacted accordingly. The next time I saw my dad was probably a couple of months later. My brother, sister, and I were in the backseat of a car, and my mom was driving. I saw my dad with a group of other men working in a ditch with swing blades and bush axes. They were all dressed the same. He was on the chain gang there in Sarasota, FL. He eventually worked his way up to trustee and became the bus driver for the chain gang. There are perks that come with being trustee. For my parents, it meant that they got to see each other often and have physical contact. For my mom, this must have been much better than just the standard visitation days where you can't touch each other. After my dad brought all the prisoners in, he'd drive the bus over to the lot and clean it. My mom would meet up with him there and give him a little bottle of whiskey when she could afford it.

Back home, things got bad really quick. My dad had been the breadwinner of the family. He even bought me my first motorcycle from Hap's when I was ten years old. In truth, he was a very hard worker. He only missed two days of work in the twelve years he worked at Moss Brothers. He missed one day to take a physical for the army and one to go to his brother-in- law's funeral. I noticed that things started to disappear. First, it was the animals. Next, I noticed that my dad's Harley Davidson motorcycles went. Anything of any value just started leaving. No more horses, no pastures, no hogs. It was all gone. We even lost our home. My mom, brother, sister and I had to move into a one-room row house in downtown Sarasota. Gone were the woods and creeks that were our familiar surroundings.

We started moving around as a way of life. We wouldn't be at one place very long. I lost count of all the different places we lived. My mom was just trying to survive. She was alone with three kids, trying to work and take care of us without enough of anything.

A few years ago, my wife and I went back to Sarasota to retrace some of the places that I did remember. We found the house where I lived at eleven years old when everything changed. I could barely handle the flood of memories that pushed themselves into my awareness. The house looked so small compared to how it looked when I was a kid. In my mind's eye I saw myself as a child, running across that yard and getting on the church bus. By the grace of God and the Holy Spirit, I felt like I had gone back in time. I spoke to that eleven year-old boy and said to him, "There're going to be some things that are going to happen around you. Some of it's not going to be pleasant, but you will get through it." I thought about Psalm 23 (NKJV):

> **1** A Psalm of David. The Lord is my shepherd; I shall not want. **2** He makes me to lie down in green pastures; He leads me beside the still waters. **3** He restores my soul; He leads me in the paths of righteousness For His name's sake. **4** Yea, though I walk through the valley of the shadow of death, I will fear no evil; For You are with me; Your rod and Your staff, they comfort me. **5** You prepare a table before me in the presence of my enemies; You anoint my head with oil; My cup runs over. **6** Surely goodness and mercy shall follow me All the days of my life; And I will dwell in the house of the Lord Forever.

I needed that little boy to know that there is hope. I needed him to know about Jesus Christ, our Savior.

My mom had a lot of boyfriends while my dad was locked up. I've been in enough hard times to know that you are likely to make different decisions when times are hard than you would if you had money. Maybe these men who were in and out of her life helped my mom not to feel so alone. Maybe they helped her with money. I think it was a little of both. I'm not trying to be too hard on her for the things she did to try to take care of her children. Even with the other men in her life, she visited my dad regularly for the three years that he was on the chain gang. As far as I know, there was no official breakup between my mom and dad. Actually, even though their relationship never was restored to what it had been before the shooting, they remained married until they were separated by death.

Some of my mom's family was also settled in Sarasota. When I was thirteen years old, I hung out with my cousins a lot. There were a lot of them and they were older, probably in their late teens, and a lot bigger than me. One of the things they would do for fun was put me and my brother, Tommy, in a circle and make us fight. It wasn't some traditional kind of fighting like judo, karate, or boxing. This was animalistic. It was like being in a pit, and you had to do whatever you could to beat the other person because they were trying to hurt you. This meant kicking, biting, scratching, whatever it took. The fight was not over until one of us could no longer stand. This mentality would characterize my fighting for years to come.

I remember one time we were all at my mom's sister Mary Jane's house. Some of the older boys I was just talking about were her sons. We were all outside in an El Camino. One of the older boys, Danny, kept putting his feet on me, and I took that as disrespect. In our world, if you felt like you were disrespected, you had to take up for yourself, or you would be seen as a coward. A couple of times, I pushed his feet off. I told him that he was a lot bigger than me, and this would not be a fair fight. Remember, I was the youngest. About the third time, I looked around the inside of the El Camino and found a paint can. I threw that can at him as hard as I could and jumped out of the truck. As my other cousins helped him into the house, I saw blood gushing from behind his ear.

Imagine the scene: We're there for a picnic and everybody's going nuts. They were pointing at me like *I* was the bad guy. My mom asked me why I did it. I explained to her that I had told him twice to take his feet off me, with no effect, so the third time I told him another way. I had such rage! I was calm and matter of fact about it. Even in my rage, I could calmly say, "I told you to keep your feet off me. Maybe now you'll listen to what I tell you." No one was going to disrespect me and not pay for it with physical pain. Not now, not ever.

As I've already said, times were tough, things were lean, and my mom was having terrible difficulty trying to take care of three kids.

One day when I was about thirteen, my mother got me and Tommy together and informed us that Tommy would be moving to Canada with his mother Carol. This was the day we found out that we really weren't brothers. My mom explained it like this: Around the same time my dad had married my mom, his brother, Wayne, married her sister Carol. The marriage between my aunt and uncle produced Tommy in 1960. Wayne and Carol split up shortly thereafter when my uncle went to jail.

During that time, my mom had gone over to my aunt's trailer and heard Tommy crying. Carol had left Tommy alone in there! So, my mom took him and raised him. Simple as that! No discussion and no paperwork. Mom just did what needed to be done. Anyway, as far as telling me when she did, I can only speculate that my mom was trying to lessen the pain of Tommy and I being separated. Maybe she thought that if I knew I was only losing a cousin, it wouldn't hurt as much. It didn't matter. To me, I was losing a brother.

CHAPTER 3

Ohio or Bust

M en came and went. I didn't want anything to do with any of them. I was still on my dad's side. I didn't want any of them hanging around, let alone trying to tell me what to do. We went to Ohio and, for a little bit, we moved in with my dad's mother. She was a Christian lady who never drank a drop in her life. I called her my little grandmother. She stood all of four foot seven and a half inches tall. She was a lady of God who didn't take any guff. I remember her as the only person who could calm me down at that time. There was something about her that was different. Later in life, I would learn that the difference in Little Grandma was Jesus Christ.

My mom and two kids moved in with Little Grandma and my Grandpa JD. He was a hard drinker. Maybe that's where my dad and uncle got it from. I remember that Little Grandma would reward me for finding where JD stashed his wine bottles, so she could pour them out. These were the days when there was still an outhouse by the creek. Let's just say he had some pretty ingenious places to hide his alcohol! He was pretty mad when he found out that I helped Little Grandma on this mission to rid their home and her husband of alcohol. I remember responding hatefully to whatever meanness he tried to dish out to me, "If you mess with me, I'll take care of you too." I don't think we had a grandfather/grandson relationship from that point on, if we ever had one in the first place.

My grandmother was set in her ways and didn't condone certain things. One of those things was my mom running with other men while she was still married to my dad, so she gave my mother an ultimatum: the drinking and carousing would have to stop. My mom took offense and moved in with some guy in town. My sister stayed with my grandmother, and I was sent off to live with some cousins in Sabina, Ohio. I was twelve years old at that time. Yes, my mom left us kids so she could run around with some man who was not my dad. I lived in Sabina for the greater part of a year.

That was yet another strained, dysfunctional household. There were three families trying to live together on one farm, and I was just one more financial burden. Nevertheless, they took me in, and I went to school. My first job where I got paid on a regular basis was as a paperboy. I loved that job! I'd get up very early, like at 4:30, and all the newspapers would be on the front door. I had to rubber band them individually, put them in the big old white bag that was provided, and deliver all of them before school started. I gave some of the money to the people taking care of me. For the first time in my life I had the good feeling that only comes from being independent, and a job did that for me.

I had learned that if you worked, you could take care of yourself and not be dependent on other people. I grew up watching my mom be subjected to things that I believe were not on her wish list, and I don't believe a lot of those things would have happened had she been financially independent. I learned that if you worked, you could have things you wanted, not just whatever you could get. My cousin and I did hang out and do some things we maybe shouldn't have-- just normal types of teenage mischief-- but I did well in school. I did very well with the paper route and felt like I was contributing to the world. I was even asked if I wanted to be on the safety patrol. Those on the safety patrol got this badge and helped people cross the street. I not only became a crossing guard, but I also got a real badge! I became a leader, making sure all the crosswalks were being taken care of properly. Things felt pretty good even though I didn't see my mom or sister very much and hadn't seen my dad for a long

13

time. I had emotionally detached from my family. I think that helped me to survive.

One day when I was about thirteen, my mom suddenly showed up and said, "We're going back to Florida." "I don't want to go back to Florida," I told her, "I have a job, and I'm helping out around here. I have status at my school. I'm not only doing OK academically, I'm the head guy in the crossing guard." I remembered all that chaos in Florida, but the decision wasn't mine, and we ended up right back in the same mess. I knew I wasn't being told everything and felt that my parents hadn't been making good decisions my whole life. I *was* making good decisions for my life, and yet my mom was interfering with the good. My good decisions seemed to be working out pretty well, and I resented her making me leave all that was good.

Off we went, back to the same old stuff, back to the Fight Club cousins. I don't know if my dad was getting out of prison soon and maybe my mom had this grandiose idea that they'd run into each other's arms or what. Obviously, her idea of what went on must have been completely different than mine. Moving around, fighting, and wearing the same clothes every day was not my idea of a good life. Again, I was faced with the schoolyard taunting. I'd say, "Yeah, I'm wearing the same clothes I did yesterday, and if you say anything I'll punch you in the mouth." Gone were the pride and independence that I had so successfully built up in Sabina.

I fought all the time for the next twenty-five years. My dad eventually got out of prison, but they would not hire him back at Moss Brothers because of the felony on his record. They wouldn't even speak to him, and that broke his spirit even more than it already was. We ended up moving from place to place, leaving each one in the middle of the night before being kicked out for not paying the rent. My parents started staying at different people's homes, and there often just wasn't room for three kids, so I went from foster home to foster home. I thought that these people were taking me in just to make a buck, and that affected how I acted toward them.

One foster home stands out in my mind because it was like a storybook family. It was a conservative, middle-class home, with prayer before healthy meals, chores for the kids, a father who went to work every day and a mother who stayed home. The house was nice and clean, with nothing broken and everything in its place. The kids went to school every day, came home and did their chores without complaint. Everybody sat at the table for dinner and discussed the day, maybe watched a little TV or played board games.

My sense of normal was as opposite as you can get from that place. I was used to loud, chaotic environments filled with arguments and fighting, drunkenness, people in and out, not enough food sometimes, and hardly any clothes to wear. I was used to no expectations on the part of parents, except that I was not to do anything that would get them in trouble. There were no discussions about current events or feelings about the day. We were just lucky when nobody was in jail and we had a place to live for any length of time.

I was very rude to my foster family. I felt like a throwaway. I don't remember any type of counseling to explain why this family looked this way and why my family looked that way. I thought, "Why don't my parents get it together so they can give me what these kids get?" I lashed out by cussing at my foster parents, not doing what I was told, and generally doing anything I could to make them stop being so kind. Everything about it was a shock to my system. You take someone from a situation like I was in and throw them into that situation, and it's like throwing a fish into an aquarium without allowing it to acclimate first. As I said, these people were very nice, but they were everything I did not get in my "normal life." I didn't deal with it that well. I knew I would be going back to that life any day, so I could not let myself get soft. Understand, that to survive in my world meant having to be street-smart and tough. Letting my guard down, receiving these people's love, would have destroyed me in my world.

That was my reality at the time, and I know that there are foster families out there right now that are going through the same experiences with a child in their home. I want them to understand that these kids want to love and be loving but might not be able to at this time. Your kindness is not "all for nothing" and does make a difference to your foster kids. Years later, I still appreciate what those people did for me. I'd like to meet those people again and talk to them. I hope I get that chance.

I remember that on a trip back to Sarasota with my wife, as we were driving around taking pictures, we pulled into a little ballpark. I shut the car off, and we just sat there for a minute. My wife remarked, "This is a pretty little park." I told her that this was one of the places I lived. Literally—not just in this neighborhood -- in our car in the park. She was shocked. I had never told her about this before. It's true; we not only lived in the worst neighborhoods, but we also lived in our car for a while. Imagine living in a Florida public park with no air conditioning and three kids in the back seat. I can imagine it was rough for my parents. I know it was rough for us kids. We eventually moved into Big Grandma's house. I never met my maternal grandpa, since he had died before I was born. I did learn that he was the fighter in the family. My mom said that I must have gotten it from him.

I think family always tries to help family, but when your resources are just enough to keep you going, you can only help so much. Money was tight, space was tight, and my mom and dad could never get their drinking under control. People had good intentions, but, just like Little Grandma in Ohio, people also had conditions. Since following any kind of rules was not my parents' forte, even though my parents were back together, we ended up living in some pretty uncomfortable places.

The last place I remember living before coming back to Ohio when I was thirteen was a trailer on someone else's property. The people we rented from had a big house with a barn and some other outbuildings, including a very small trailer. There was just one little bed in it. Everything about it was little, but there was one good thing: we were surrounded by woods. We could just get lost in them, which we found to be a welcome escape. There were great big vines, and I would just swing on them like Tarzan. We had pastures next to us, complete with horses. I used to ride on them bareback just for something to do. We had a place to live, woods to play in, and animals around us. In a way, my parents had managed to get back some of what we had before my dad shot that man. Our family of five lived in that little trailer for a time. Mom and dad were trying to work, but there was always the drinking.

On the other side of us was a skeet shooting range. I got a job there. My job was to sit in the concrete bunker and load the machine that threw the clay pigeons. Talk about a hectic job! There would be five shooters lined up and a guy standing behind them who controlled the switch. Whenever the arm of the skeet launcher came back, I'd have to load it. Sometimes, they played doubles, and I had to load with both arms simultaneously! This meant going through a box of clay pigeons in no time. The trick was to try to get another box open while loading with both hands. Sometimes, these guys would be drinking and shooting, and if there was nothing in the machine when they yelled, "Pull!" it made them mad, and they'd shoot the back of the box where I was sitting. Sometimes I'd imagine that it was WWII, and I was a soldier in a bunker who was under fire. In a way, my whole life seemed like a battle.

When that job ended, I went to work at a nursing home with my dad. It was 1974, and I was thirteen years old. My dad was the janitor at the nursing home that borders the Bobby Jones Golf Course in Sarasota. It was one of the places my wife and I found on our trip. I had worked there as my dad's assistant, running the floor buffer and wax stripper. I really liked that job. Any time I had a job, I had the feeling of independence that comes from making your own money. I encourage my children to work hard because I want them to feel it, too. If you have a job, you don't have to sit with your hand out, waiting for someone to take care of you. You're not at someone else's mercy.

An old guy in the nursing home named Irv used to sell pop to the golfers. They knew he was there at a certain time every day and it sort of became my job to help him. I would get his cooler and his ice. Irv had a little spot at the fence. The golfers would come over to the fence and buy cans of pop from him. He treated me like a grandson or maybe even a son. We got to be really close to each other.

I came to work one day with nothing particular on my mind. It was just another day at work, or so I thought. Once I got inside, one of the workers pulled me off to the side and sat me down. I noticed that everyone was being really quiet and wore strange expressions on their faces. I knew I wasn't in trouble; the look wasn't like that. I'd been in trouble enough; I knew what the *in trouble* look was. This was something less familiar-a *feeling sorry for me* look. One of the workers put their hand on my shoulder and said, "Well, Irv died." I knew about death, but it had never been this close to me. Irv's death created a hole in me. Something close to me was gone. I had no concept of heaven or hell, no concept that the person would always be alive as long as they were in my heart. Still, it's forty years later, and here I am speaking about him now because he is alive in my heart. I pray that he received Jesus Christ as his savior before he died. If that happened, I know I'll see him again.

At that time, I didn't know all that. So many things ran through my head. I felt cheated. I felt abandoned. I felt sorry for myself. I felt angry. At about that time, I started running around with some boys in the neighborhood who lived around the corner from me. We started getting into some things we shouldn't have. My dad got into some trouble and ended up on the chain gang again. My mom, my brother Tommy, my sister, and I were alone again and I got into things I shouldn't have. I started missing work. I showed up to work one day, and I learned a new word: terminated. I didn't even know what that meant. They had to explain it to me. My job was over, and I blamed everyone around me for what had happened. I was not able to process what was going on in my life, and I had nobody to help me process it. So, I just reacted. I reacted with whatever I had in me at that time. I was a walking time-bomb.

Eventually, my dad got out of jail again and life went on. One day, my friends and I discovered that one of the outbuildings on the property where my parents rented the trailer had some cool stuff in it. We thought there were guns in there, so we broke into it one night, only to learn that we were wrong. We found ammunition, gunpowder, big cans of black powder, and some other stuff, but no guns. In keeping with our typical craftiness, we found a way to make our discovery exciting. We started blowing stuff up with it. We just took it out into the woods, put the stuff on the stump, lit it up, and hunkered down under the stump, waiting for the bullets to go off. On one of these occasions, one of the boys raised up before everything had exploded. Just then, one of the shells went off, somehow sending the shell casing toward him and messing up his hand.

This injury wasn't something you could take care of with a Band-Aid. The boy had to go to his mom and dad, who took him to the ER. Naturally, they wanted to know what happened and questioned the boy. As you might know, it's not hard to get information out of a thirteen-year-old kid. The whole story came out, and it led back to my friends and me. Apparently, the landlord got wind of this, because he approached my mom and dad about it. All I know is, there was a fight, and we were forcibly removed from the property at gunpoint.

CHAPTER 4

School Days

It was about a year after the big tornado of '74, and once again we on our way back to Ohio to stay at Little Grandma's house. That meant living with my Grandpa JD again, and I wasn't looking forward to that. Once we got there, I was enrolled at Warner Middle School, since the tornado had leveled Central Middle School, where I would have attended. A lot of people had gotten hurt in that tornado. A year later, they were still trying to rebuild Central, so they put some trailers on the property at Warner to accommodate the extra students. I had some classes in the trailers; I had some classes in the main building. My heart wasn't in it, though. After being ripped from the success I had built in Sabina, I just sort of gave up. I had no support, no one to guide me. I was just thirteen, and I didn't have the skills to cope with the chaos that was my life.

School was indoors, where I felt trapped. I didn't want to do things inside. I wanted to do things outside. Just like at the nursing home where I cut grass and worked for Irv, I struggled with authority. I knew that I needed a job, and that I needed to be outside. At that age, all I knew was: "I do this, and I feel good; I do that, and I do not." Being outside made me feel good. My capacity to process life was limited, but I knew that sitting inside a classroom and being told what to do did not work for me. I was in seventh grade four times. During that time, I got shuffled around a lot. I think they were just trying to make it work for their system; I didn't care. There were a couple of years there where you could have added up the number of days I went to school on one hand. As I said before, when it came right down to it, my parents told me they didn't really care what I did as long as it didn't come back on them.

Eventually, skipping school, also known as *truancy*, was one of those things that came back on my parents. So I had to go to school, but what I did once I got there was up to me. I did things to get put out of school. Fighting worked really well. Sure, the paddling hurt but only for a short time. I had learned in the Fight Club that being hit hurt, but only for a time. There were a couple of teachers and an assistant principal who tried to prove me wrong. I remember a shop teacher who tried to teach me something. He just lit me up! Talk about your feet coming up off the floor. It hurt, and I cried, but once he stopped hitting me, I'd cuss him out and say, "Is that all you can do? You like hitting little boys?" My behavior was well within the boundaries my parents had set for me. If taking some pain for a little while is what it took to get out of the classroom, that's what I did.

I started smoking cigarettes at a very young age. I picked up my dad's cigarettes at the age of eleven. I'd go to school, sit in the hallway on one of the heat registers and light up a cigarette, waiting for a teacher to show up. Eventually, one of them would ask me what I was doing. I'd say, "What does it look like I'm doing? I'm smoking a cigarette." They'd get this look of shock on their face for a minute, and then tell me that I couldn't do that at school. I'd come back with, "Looks like I can. I'm doing it right now." You see, I knew that if I got suspended four times there would be a meeting with the district superintendent. I would then be expelled for half a year. I had learned that I could get put out of school for a lot less pain this way. Since they didn't beat me with a paddle for smoking, I'd just do that "smoking in the hallway routine" all over again to get expelled for another half year.

It was the first year after they had rebuilt Central Middle School. I remember trying to succeed at school that year, both physically and mentally. I don't know what made me want to try, but try I did! I was bigger than a lot of the boys I went to school with. I had broad

21

shoulders. I remember trying out for football and whizzing through all that with ease. I don't think I would have been a quarterback, but maybe a linebacker. Unfortunately for me, I had long hair. I also had the idea that, "This is who I am. If you don't like it, that's your problem." The coach said, "You'll have to cut that hair off." I don't know if he meant it, but what I heard was, "I don't like that long hair. If you don't cut it off, you can't be on the team." I told him, "I don't have to do nothin'."

There was a game we played back then called Smear the Queer. It was sort of like Chicken. I remember this boy named Greg Ward. He was the coach's star football player, and he was no coward. During one game of Smear the Queer, I saw Greg holding the ball. I took my shot, and I hit him hard. You know, I didn't have anything against him. I had something against the coach. Anyway, I hurt him, and he couldn't play anymore. He sprained either his ankle or wrist. I remember the coach coming up to me and cussing me out. He put his hands on me and told me what a loser I was for messing up his football player. I sneered, "How do you like my long hair now?" If he could have, I believe he'd have beat me to death right then. My football days were over for a while. Later on, I picked it back up when I was in the penitentiary. It's somewhat ironic, looking back, that it was prison that gave me the opportunity to play- not my school.

Anyway, I remember trying academically that year, working with counselors. I had a couple of female teachers who really cared about me. I don't know if it was that they wanted to be my mom, or more that I wanted them to be my mom. Either way, there was some kind of connection that felt warm and good like a mother's love should. One was a science teacher, and the other, a civics teacher. I did really well that year. I even made the honor roll one quarter! I still felt like a thug, but I also felt good.

My mom and dad had taken me with them to bars from a very early age. Maybe back then, in the neighborhoods where we lived, this was not looked upon as wrong. One bar my mom attended pretty regularly was called The Depot. It was on the same grounds as the train depot in Xenia. Nowadays, Xenia is a big bicycling community, and the depot serves as a bicycle trail hub. But back then, it was a bar and my mom would take me in with her. A lot of times, if she met the right person, she would leave me downstairs in the bar with whoever was there while she went upstairs with the guy. There were rooms upstairs. Some people might think, "Well that's just awful, taking her son to bars while she took men upstairs." But that's not the point of the story. The point is that I didn't see anything wrong with it. Besides, I liked all the attention that I was getting from these females. I had already "been with" a woman back in Sarasota so I knew how good it felt. I didn't think there was anything wrong with what my mom was doing. I just thought it was the way people lived.

We were out one night when my mom picked up some guy. We drove out on Stove Rd., which is in the country. I was told to get out of the car and hang out while my mom and this guy took care of business. I wish I could remember what was going through my head at the time, but all I know is that I really didn't think there was anything wrong going on. After they finished up, my mom came out and told me that she was going to take this guy's money and his car. She told me to just stand there, and she would do all the talking. When he got out of the car, they exchanged words. The next thing I know, he is backing away from the car, we're getting in, and driving on down the road into Xenia. I found out later that she had used me as a bargaining tool. Remember, I was a big kid for my age and probably looked intimidating. I remember thinking, "This is crazy." I had been in trouble before, but not something like this and not with my mom. I have no idea why she did this crap. We parked the car somewhere; she tried to wipe her fingerprints off; and we went home.

The next day the police showed up, arresting both of us for strong-armed robbery and auto theft. So there I was, fifteen years old and sitting in Greene County Juvenile Detention. Talk about not liking the inside! There I was, sitting on a tiny mattress not knowing what's going on, and all I could think about was that I was going to miss finals testing at school. As it turned out, while I was locked up, one of the guidance counselors from Central brought every one of those tests to me! It was just awesome. It got my mind off of things,

23

and I not only passed the ninth grade, it was the best year I ever had in school. I had passed on my own!

I was released to be with my dad until all this legal stuff got straightened out. A few days later, the police came and got me. My mom was already in their cruiser. They were there to drive us to the Bureau of Criminal Investigation, or BCI, in London, Ohio. The BCI facility is on the same grounds as London Correctional Institution, which is a big work farm. As we approached the grounds, I couldn't help but notice what looked like a huge medieval castle. The men I could see were all dressed the same. At fifteen years old, I was seeing London Correctional Institution, and it was totally overwhelming.

We had been taken to BCI for lie detector tests. My mom went in, and, after what seemed like an eternity, came out crying. They never tested me. My mom had told them that she had forced me into the robbery and that I had nothing to do with it. As a result, I got out of it with no charges at all. My mom pleaded guilty and was sentenced to a year in Marysville prison. My dad had been to prison, now my mom was in prison, and it wasn't too long before I was following in their footsteps. About seven years later, I would find myself inside that big medieval prison doing a fifteen-year sentence. Some people grow up expecting that they are going to go to college for four years, get a good job, get married, and then start a family. Well, those aren't the expectations that I was raised with, and to me, my life was normal. My life was mostly uncomfortable and often painful, but I didn't think any of it was out of the ordinary. It was just the way life was. It was what was expected.

CHAPTER 5

Bar's Bottom

I ended up moving deeper into criminal activity. I advanced to another level of credibility with the people I hung around with in a section of town called Bar's Bottom. Bar's Bottom was a dead end street that ended in a creek that runs through Xenia. I loved spending time outside in the creek, catching crawdads and leaches that we'd fish with, and inner tubing down the river. Quite often, my friends and I would walk three or four miles to the bridge outside of Xenia to go tubing. We'd catch fish, cook them on a fire, and spend the night out there. We were always pushing the boundaries.

We weren't always doing bad things, but we did do bad things. Some things were pretty scary. There was a spot by The Depot where the winos would sleep. We knew if we went down there at certain times, it would be really dark. There were places where it was so dark that even *I* didn't go to alone. We'd go down in a group, walk down there and hear them snoring. They'd just be there sleeping in the weeds. We went down there mainly to get their wine. We'd walk right up on them lying there sleeping, reach down, take that wine bottle out of their hand, and sometimes they'd wake up. You had to be ready to bolt. We knew if they got a hold of us, they were going to beat us-- not just because we'd steal their wine, but because after we got done with the wine, we'd get handfuls of rocks, and "rock" the winos. In fact, this rocking the winos was a typical kid activity in my neighborhood. We loved doing things that got our adrenaline going, and rocking the winos was good for that.

I was never really into stealing. I was more into the "in your face" stuff, like rocking the winos. Sure, I was around some guys sometimes while they were stealing things like bikes, but I always felt that stealing was beneath me. Through my whole criminal career, I was never big into stealing. Later in life, I did forcibly take things from people, but it was for a reason-- like collecting on a debt.

At the end of my ninth grade school year, we were living right across from what was the Foosball Palace in Xenia. I had done well in school that year, and I was proud of myself for that. Anyhow, all the cool kids went to the Foosball Palace, but they had to be brought in from the nice part of town. This was downtown Xenia, where people like me lived. In fact, we lived in a one-bedroom upstairs apartment across the street. One night, my parents were drinking and arguing with the neighbor. We wound up outside. I was sixteen years old and six foot one. Yet again, I was drawn into a situation that had been started by my mom and dad.

I ended up beating a thirty-six year old man pretty bad. I wore him out. Later on, while sitting in juvenile court, I saw that man with his face all beat up. There was not even a scratch on me. Even though my parents started the fight, only I went to jail. Sometimes I wonder if someone should have noticed that I was a kid who needed help instead of just incarcerating me. I hope the system has improved since then. Anyway, they sent me to Buckeye Youth Center on Broad St. in Columbus, Ohio. At this time, the juvenile system did not have predetermined sentencing. They had different degrees. I don't know how it works now, but that is how it was. There were several facilities that had different degrees. Buckeye was second from the top. The Training Institute of Central Ohio (TICO) was on top. That was the worst place they could send you, and Buckeye Youth Center (BYC) was on the same grounds as TICO. There was just a football field between us. We could look over and see TICO when we went outside to play football. They would threaten to send you to TICO if you got in trouble at BYC. There's always someplace worse they can send you.

They would tell you when you first showed up that you would be there for a minimum of three months. There were different stages you could work through to get your alert (their word for completing the program and being released). If you did your programming, finished all your courses, and didn't get any write-ups, you got your alert. Well, due to fighting, smoking, and just being a pain in their side, my ninety-day minimum went to two weeks shy of a year. I was there for eleven months and two weeks. I don't know how many times I lost my alert because of repeatedly messing up. I was recommended to be sent to TICO more than once. One time it was for inciting a riot in the chow hall. I had started a fight between my clique and another clique there. I spent my seventeenth birthday in the Buckeye Youth Center. That was the first birthday I ever spent in jail.

I was released in October of 1979, and spent my eighteenth birthday out. I started carrying a gun around with me. Like I said, my parents really weren't concerned as long as it didn't bring them any trouble. I had learned in Sabina that having a job meant independence. Ever since then, I always had some sort of legitimate job, no matter what else I was involved in. I wasn't a thief; I was just aggressive. One night, I was with my mom and dad in a little local bar. They were getting sauced up pretty good. I left to drive around and drink some beer with one of the neighborhood girls I ran with, who had an El Camino. I figured I should go back to the bar to check on things.

The girl and I went back, parked in the alley, and I went in. My dad was up in somebody's face. I got in the middle of the situation and told my mom we'd better leave before someone got hurt. I remember putting my dad's hand on the butt of my gun. I saw a shocked, knowing look come over my dad's face-like maybe he knew something really bad was about to happen. Now that I think about it, it was one of the few times I saw any expression when he was in an alcohol-induced stupor. Apparently, when I said, "Let's get out of here before someone gets hurt," my statement was taken as a threat that I was going to hurt the people in the bar. Even today, people sometimes make assumptions about me because my voice carries and sounds a certain way. As we were trying to leave the bar, the owner and the bouncer followed us out into a really confined space where I felt trapped. I know that feeling of being trapped played into what happened next. We got into a confrontation in the alley behind the bar.

I wound up shooting one of the guys that followed us out. I never really got excited about it. I never have gotten excited about situations like that. It's how I was raised. You just dealt with things as they came at you. Everybody else got excited, though. The owner was shot, and his bouncer dragged him back inside the bar. The girl in the El Camino became hysterical, screaming, "You just shot somebody!" over and over. I told her to scoot over so I could drive. My parents took off in their car. I drove the El Camino to my house and told the girl to go home. I reassured her that nothing would happen to her since she didn't do anything wrong. She left, and I went to the fridge, got a beer, and sat by the window to wait for the inevitable. Our house sat on a hill, in a group of double-wide trailers on Stelton Road, so I could see pretty well down the street. I never was big on running. I didn't know exactly what was going to happen, but I knew I had nowhere to run. Besides, running wasn't part of who I was.

Once I saw the first cruiser outside, I have to admit I felt a little of what I know now was *fight or flight*. I went down in the basement and got under a tarp. Now that I think about it, it wasn't a very good hiding place. It wasn't long before I heard the sound of footsteps clomping down the wooden stairway leading to the basement. I found out later that between the city police, highway patrol, and sheriffs, there were over twenty officers in the house. For all they knew, I still had the gun. They were loaded for a bear. All they knew was that they were after someone who had just shot someone in the mouth. I heard my mom crying and screaming, "Don't kill him." Then, I heard this really calm, controlled voice say, "We're going to pull this tarp back, and if you move, I'm going to shoot you." Someone was standing over me with their feet on either side of me at chest level, pointing a shotgun at me.

I later learned that my feet were sticking out from under the tarp. He asked me if I still had the gun. He told me not to make any sudden moves, and I didn't. I can definitely follow directions when absolutely necessary. He continued talking me through the process. The barrel of his gun looked like as big around as a can of green beans, it was so big. I told him that I had thrown my gun outside the bar. They searched me, took me down to the car and got me to the police station. They booked me in the city jail, brought me back, and started giving me details about what I had done. By then, they had reports back from the hospital.

When I shot this guy, it was a .22 caliber bullet, but it was a special bullet they'd come out with just a few months before. It was a Stinger, and it did exactly what it was designed to do. The bullet went through his top lip and knocked two of his front teeth out. Then, the hollow point fragmented and ricocheted on the bone in the roof of his mouth, exiting from his ear. "It doesn't look good," they said. "It looks like he's going to die." I sat alone, feeling trapped and thinking about the situation. "Looks like I've killed somebody," I thought. I somehow went to sleep that night, but the thought of having killed someone never left my awareness. I had finally gotten to the top tier of things that I thought were top tier, anyway. I had actually shot someone and killed them.

CHAPTER 6

Calm, Cool and Collected

I remember sitting on the bunk in that jail cell, eighteen years old, all alone, just being told that this man that I shot was probably going to die. Yet, in the face of crisis I stayed calm, just as I had learned to do as a matter of survival from a very young age. My mentality was simply, "OK, this is happening now, deal with it." I was cold inside, and would stay that way for many years. All the things that had been done to me, all the things I had been a part of had turned me into this *thing* that didn't have a whole lot of feelings. Maybe I had feelings, but I knew how quickly I could be hurt, so I locked them away. It was safer that way.

As it turned out, the man I shot in the face survived. Considering the severity of the wound, the prosecutor charged me with attempted murder. I didn't have any money, so I didn't get what we called a real lawyer. I got a "yes man" from the county.

I know now that there are some good lawyers who do pro bono work, but I didn't know that at the time. I found out that they wanted to charge me with attempted murder. My jailhouse advisors told me that there's no way they could charge me with that, since I didn't even know the man. I already knew from my time at Buckeye Youth Center that there's always a plea deal offered. I had once been told by a reliable source that if everybody charged with a felony requested a jury trial in any county, the county would be broke in thirty days-they just couldn't afford it. So, they made deals.

What's so scary about deals made with the prosecutor is that they involved standing up before the judge and publicly say that no one told you how to plead or made any guarantees about sentencing. Usually judges went along with it, because they wanted people to cooperate, and that wouldn't happen if they didn't hold up their end of the bargain.

After some back and forth between my public defender and the prosecutor, they came in with a deal. They said, "We'll let you cop out. We'll let you plead guilty to felonious assault, and you'll get a max of fifteen years. As long as you don't catch another case while you're in prison, the longest they can keep you is fifteen years. If you don't take that, then we will try you for aggravated felonious assault, which carries a max of twenty-five years." That was their way-to scare you with the prospect of a maximum sentence while offering a less painful option. After back and forth with my lawyer, I took the plea deal.

I pleaded guilty to felonious assault and was given a prison term not to exceed fifteen years. During the time I was in the county jail, I had become friends with the other guys that were in there. I got pretty close to two of them. They had already been to prison once, so they were giving me the low down on the two prisons where I'd be incarcerated. Ohio State Reformatory in Mansfield, Ohio was the first place I'd go. They knew that because of where I lived, I'd end up there and then go to London Correctional Institution. As was typical back then, after I was convicted and sentenced I was sent on to my destination in under a week. At that time, there were certain things that determined where you would do your time. One of those things was age; the other was your number of convictions. If you were under thirty and this was your first felony conviction, you went to a reformatory. If you were under the age of thirty and had more than one felony conviction, you went to a penitentiary. If you were over the age of thirty and it was your first conviction, you went to a penitentiary. Anybody above the age of thirty was going to the penitentiary.

Being eighteen years of age and a first time loser, I was bound for the reformatory. I was given a reformatory number-112421, a number I would never forget. One day I would get a penitentiary number-178143, but that would come later. At the time of my sentencing, there were two primary reformatories in Ohio: Ohio State Reformatory (OSR), Mansfield, Ohio and Lebanon Correctional Institution (LCI), in between Dayton and Cincinnati. What determined which of these two facilities you would be sent to was the county where you were convicted. Visualize an imaginary line drawn right through the center of the state. If you were convicted above the line, you went to OSR. If you were convicted below the line, you went to Lebanon Correctional. I was convicted below the line, so I would be doing my time at LCI. At that time, OSR was the receiving center for all reformatory inmates, so I got to do time in both facilities.

Usually at the county jail, they would transport prisoners in groups of two or three, but with me that was not the case. They transferred me by myself. Believe it or not, just getting out of jail and riding in a car was a treat, even if it was the backseat of a sheriff's car. I felt unhealthy. I had been lying in the county jail with no access to the outside. When you're going to prison, at least you know you're going to get out on the yard. That day in July, the weather was actually nice, and the sun was out. The deputies and I chit chatted like buddies the whole way there. I remember joking with them about passing people. It seemed like they passed a lot of cars on the road that day. I said something jokingly like, "You know, we're not in a race or anything, so you can take your time." Nervous chatter. They did their best to prepare me, but no words alone can describe what I felt as I got closer to the Ohio State Reformatory in Mansfield. I was overcome with a sense of dread. This place was, and still is, intimidating to look at. They took me inside receiving, wished me luck and went on their way. While I waited with twenty or so other men, I thought about those fifteen years. People already in the system had told me that I'd better be expecting to do the whole fifteen years. I was now in the hands of the State of Ohio Corrections Department.

When the Ohio State Reformatory was built in 1886, the idea was to give first-time offenders a humane place to change their ways. Unfortunately, as the prison's life went on over its 94 years of existence, it became a place known for torture, inhumane conditions, and even murder. Shut down in 1990, the prison is now a prime site for ghost hunters who believe that the restless spirits of inmates mistreated there still walk the halls. (Information taken from Explore History & Haunting at the Ohio State Reformatory. 2014. Retrieved from http://www.mrps.org/)

Standing in front of the tall, castle-like building, you might never guess that prisoners were exposed to deplorable conditions here, including rats, disease, violence from other prisoners, and punishments like solitary confinement in The Hole. *The Hole* was an area of confinement cells with only a bunk and a toilet where as many as 120 prisoners could be in an area with only 20 rooms. This prison was no longer the sanctuary for reform that it had been designed to be. It was a dangerous torture chamber where you learned that your life was worth nothing and that your only chance for survival was to toughen up and look out for yourself. (Information taken from Mansfield Reformatory. n.d. Retrieved June 2, 2014 from http://www.deadohio.com/mansfieldreformatory.htm)

CHAPTER 7

Rude Awakening

I learned quickly that the guards weren't my friends, and they didn't care what my name was. From that moment on, and for the next six years, I was 112421 or 178143. They stripped me down and rid me of anything that resembled freedom. As was standard procedure, they took away anything that would remind me of the outside world, like rings, watches, and even my shoes. They deloused me. We were all made to wear dark blue pants and black boots that were made in the prison. Looking around, I noticed that we all looked exactly the same.

The guards kept us in a sally port until they got a group of six to eight inmates. A sally port is a room that separates one area from another. In this case, it was a place to contain you after receiving you into the prison and before taking you into the actual cellblock. They had just emptied the room out, finished up with me, and put me in the port to wait. There I was again, alone in a room with a steel door on either side of me. One door led to the outside world, and one door led to the prison. I could hear it. I could even feel it-- a kind of electricity coming from the prison side of the room. Try to picture this: 2200 men locked up in cages for twenty-three hours a day. The front of the cells are open, and by that, I mean there were bars on the front of the cells, but there was nothing to stop the noise. And any minute, I was going to be thrown into that environment.

I think they intentionally make any door to any kind of jail or prison loud. I do prison ministry now, and I still look around when they are doing anything with the doors. The sound of their huge keys working those big tumblers startles me to this day. Sitting there by myself, I wondered, "What in the world have I gotten myself into?" There were no tears or fear. Looking back now, I believe I was trying to formulate some kind of plan to get through this. I knew any plan was better than no plan.

After a while, two prison guards walked a guy into the room and left him with me. He was six five and 260 lbs. His arms looked eighteen inches around. Blood gushed out of his head. I later found out that someone had caught him sleeping and piped him as payback for some offense. Although size can help you in some situations in prison, it is no guarantee of safety. If someone wants to hurt you, they will find a way. That was my first view of what lay in store for me beyond that closed door. There was violence and survival of the fittest was the rule. Just to survive, you had to have physical or mental fitness, but it was best to have both. As I went through the door, I went with the same thought that helped me survive the "fight club" so many years before. We had a saying, "You can beat me, but you can't eat me." There was a sense of finality as the door to the free world clanged shut.

My first night at OSR was spent in the hospital, along with all the other incoming inmates. As part of in-processing, they shave off all your hair. When you get there, there are people who have big afros, long hair, or beards, but they come out looking so different that you can't recognize them. The room was filled with row upon row of beds. My first night, I ended up getting a bed by the wall where I could look out a window. I remember that just being able to look out this window and look into the night sky gave me some relief from being in this place. Indeed, those on the outside looking up at the stars would have said it was a beautiful night.

There were forty to fifty of inmates in this room. One inmate seemed to have some sort of mental problem. Looking back, I know that he was very weak and shouldn't have been with us. As I lay there in my bed, I heard the awful sounds of him being molested. I heard the cries and the begging but felt no feelings of compassion. With everything that I had seen so far-from the county jail up to this moment-I had come the conclusion that there was no middle ground. You were either a taker or a giver. You were either a predator or prey. I made the decision that night that I was not going to let what had been done to this guy be done to me. All I could think about was preparing myself for survival in this predatory cesspool.

The next day, they took us to the cellblocks. The first place I was sent was 2 Southeast. They would start you out there. Then, they would move you through up to 3 Southeast, 4 Southeast, 5 Southeast, to 6 Southeast, then to 6 Northeast. By the time you were done with 6 Northeast, they sent you wherever you were classified to go. Since I was convicted in Greene County, a county below the line, I knew I would be sent to Lebanon. People convicted up north would be classified to stay at OSR.

My first night in the cellblocks, it was horribly loud. That's something I'll never, ever, ever forget. I wound up being in five institutions in Ohio, some of them more than once. The chronology looks like this: Ohio State Reformatory, Lebanon Correctional Facility, Ohio State Reformatory, Lebanon Correctional Facility, old Ohio Penitentiary in Columbus, OH (now torn down), Lebanon Correctional Facility, London Correctional Work Farm, and Orient Pre-Release.

Out of all the prisons where I did time, this was the loudest by far. There was screaming and hollering any time of day or night. There were 600 inmates just on one side of the cellblock! There were only about 18 to 24 inches between the front of the cells and the edge of the range. A range is what the walkway outside the cells is called. The range used to be open, but people would throw people off of it, so they finally put rabbit wire up, and that made it even more closed-in looking. The cells were open-faced. The open-faced cells succeeded in keeping inmates physically separate, but it did nothing to impede their constant arguing. They'd yell things like, "I'm gonna take care of you when I'm out...". I thought it was silly, knowing that if they are not going to the same prison they'll never see each other. It was just talk.

As I said, we were locked up twenty-three hours a day. We would go to the chow hall three times a day Monday through Friday and twice a day on Saturday and Sunday. I remember my first trip to the chow hall. They herded us across the yard. I noticed some people eating really quickly- just shoveling it in. I was looking at the slop, trying to see what was in it. I was busy moving it around my plate with a fork, when a guard came over and slammed his night stick on the table, barking, "You're done eating." So, I missed my first meal. You never know, maybe it was a blessing.

The official shower was once a week. They would take one range at a time-that's 100 men. We'd walk from our cells dressed in nothing but a towel and shower shoes, down the range and then an open steel spiral staircase. That staircase was very steep. You had to be very careful walking up and down it in those shower shoes. It was an easy place for accidents to happen. Really, there are a lot of places in an old prison like OSR to get hurt.

Just like for meals, they herded us onto the shower room like cattle. There was a long pipe that ran the length of the ceiling. It had showerheads every foot or so. We had just 5 minutes to get wet, soap up, and rinse off. There was no sense being bashful. Some inmates never got used to it, but I never had a problem with it, to be honest. You had to throw modesty out the window very quickly.

That doesn't mean that I didn't find ways around some things. I told the people I took on a tour to OSR, that people like to joke about not dropping the soap in the shower. One of the first things I did when I got there was to take a bar of soap, make a hole in the center of it, and tie a couple shoelaces together to make a "soap on a rope." Maybe I didn't have a problem with modesty, but that's not to say I necessarily wanted to be bending over to retrieve lost soap in a room full of 100 imprisoned men.

Out of all the things I could take from Mansfield, this is the one I talk about more than any other. It wasn't about anything physical that happened; although, there was plenty of that. It was the stone steps

37

that led up and down from the cell blocks. There was no elevator to take you from one range to another. I didn't notice it until I was up at fifth or sixth range. Two or three times a day we went up and down this stone stairway. From what I can remember, the steps were four feet wide. They were made of stone and there was a dip in them where they had been worn down from friction. I was obsessed about looking at them. I was thinking, "How many steps does it take to do this to stone? How many men have walked up and down these steps?" It was about more than the physical footsteps. In my mind, I kept picturing men hunched over, just trudging up and down these stairs. Day after day, year after year, just wearing out those stairs.

After a few months there, it was time for me to move on. It takes a few months to get through that whole process. They had a system. Once you hit 6 Northeast, you'd have two or three weeks before leaving for your classified location. For me, that was Lebanon. I was told by a couple of guys that Lebanon was a little better. Let me tell you, you deal with the same stuff in every one of them.

The day came for me to be transported to Lebanon Correctional Institution with thirty other guys. First, they took us through out-processing. We bagged up our stuff, put on bright orange jumpsuits, and boarded the bus. Most people have seen one going down the road at one time or another. If you look closely, you will see that the windows have shutters on them angled so inmates can see outside but the public can't see in.

What you can't see from the outside is that the inmates are shackled to the bus. Shackles are placed on the hands, feet, and around the waist of each inmate. Another chain secures them to the floor. Once chained to this eyelet, there's no getting loose. We talked about what would happen to us if we got in a wreck. I said, "We're going to burn up; that's what's going to happen."

We thought we were going to a better place. We were on that bus a couple of hours, having a good time and just happy to be out of the horrible place called Mansfield. Once we got to Lebanon and they stripped us down, I remember thinking, "This isn't any better than that horrible place we just left."

CHAPTER 8

Prisons: They're All Bad

After being in five prisons, each of them different from the other, I guess you could say I earned the right to my opinion on them. They were all bad. Imagine it-the name you were given by your parents is suddenly no longer your name. Your name is now a number. You have become the property of the State of Ohio. *I* was the property of the State of Ohio. From this prison to those that followed, I would get written up numerous times for violating the rules and regulations of whatever facility I was in.

When you first get to a prison and are taken into the receiving unit, you are told all their rules and regulations. I never could understand some of the rules, and of course I had that problem with authority. For example, if you got a sunburn while you were in there, you had to go to the hospital where you would get treatment. After that, they would write you up for destroying state property. They'd do the same for tattoos. They took lots of pictures of you, so if they caught you with something new they'd write you up for destroying state property.

After they tell you the rules in receiving, you go through a gambit of tests of things like your IQ and coordination. They review what your charges are. Those things determined where you were going to sleep and what job you'd have. They trained us to get out of our cells very quickly and put our toes on the line. They had us practice this a couple of times until they thought we had it. I remember that there was this big corn-fed guard with this AR-24 stick, walking and smacking his hand with it. He told us that if we read the name of this prison we would notice that it did not say "Lebanon Rehabilitation Institution". Instead, it said, "Correctional Institution". He said, "We are not here to rehabilitate you, we are here to correct you. We are to house you for the State of Ohio." I heard it, but I don't think I heard it the way I hear it now. True to its name, there was not a whole lot of emphasis on how we were going to act when we got out or how we'd be usable to society. There is a big difference between rehabilitation and correction.

Penitentiaries are considered correctional institutions. I spent some time in what was the oldest such prison in Ohio, which opened in 1834 and was called the Ohio State Penitentiary. Though the construction had not been completed at that time, the first inmates were made to build their own stone cell blocks. In its early days, the prison had a wall that went around the entire prison area, and it seemed, as time went on, that no one really cared about what went on inside the walls, as long as it didn't affect anyone on the outside. By 1893, the prison, designed to hold 1,500 inmates, was crowded with 1,900. Unfortunately, despite the growing spread of disease and violence for those incarcerated there, the prison was continually touted as a great Ohio landmark and as an example of what incarceration should be. As publicity grew, so did the prison's population, eventually peaking in 1955 when the complex was home to 5,235 inmates.

The penitentiary was home to many famous criminals- including one who claimed to be a vampire and drank his victim's blood, a confederate cavalry general, famous authors like O. Henry and Chester Himes, and even Dr. Sam Sheppard, the inspiration for *The Fugitive*. While the stories of these men are different in many ways, they all shared in the disease-infested, dangerous, overcrowded prison conditions.

Life was so difficult that the Ohio Penitentiary was home to two major riots. Each riot ended with prisoners and guards dead. When fire broke out in the prison in 1930, some guards refused to open prison blocks, leaving hundreds of men to die. A riot eventually ensued and National Guardsmen were called in to help the prison guards to keep the peace.

Once again, a prison designed originally to deter prisoners from committing crimes because of the hard work and difficult conditions, became, instead a breeding ground for harder, more skilled, career criminals. (Information taken from The Ohio Penitentiary. n.d. Retrieved June 2, 2014 from http://forgottenoh.com/Counties/ Franklin/pen.html)

That was certainly true for me, because it was in prison that I really started to come into my own as far as physical abilities. I've always been strong, but, as I said that first night in Mansfield, I was not going to be one of those weak people. I figured that one of the quickest things I could do was put some muscle on my 160 lb. frame and put tattoos on those muscles. I went from age nineteen and 163 lbs. to 228 lbs at age twenty-five, benching over 400 lbs. With that and prison tattoos all over me, I felt that I had succeeded in accomplishing the task that I set out to do all those years ago lying in the hospital in Mansfield.

You know, I've talked about being in five different prisons in Ohio. The system is set up for inmates who are sentenced to maximum security right from court. They can work their way from maximum security to medium security and from there to minimum security through good behavior. The other side of that coin is that you can start out in minimum security and end up in medium or maximum security due to behavioral infractions. In other words, inmates were moved from one place to another depending on how they acted.

I started out in maximum and even earned my way to lower levels of security more than once, but eventually I'd get into it with someone and end up in a fight. That's why I went through so many prisons, because of my aggression. I had a real problem with authority and used any means necessary to establish my dominance over others at all times. Remember, there are only two choices in prison: predator and prey, and I wasn't going to be someone's prey.

Eventually, I made it to the final leg of my prison term and was paroled. Usually, once you are paroled, it takes about thirty days before you are actually released. In between being told you are paroled and released, you are sent to a pre-release center. Ohio's pre-release center was in Orient, Ohio. There, they try to prepare you for getting out of prison. They do this by teaching you how to do things like fill out a resume and get a social security card. These were things that some of us didn't know how to do. They really did try to help us become ready to assimilate back into society at the pre-release center, but assimilating is so much more than just learning how to fill out some forms.

CHAPTER 9

London Correctional Institution, aka "The Work Farm"

L ondon is one of the work farms for the state of Ohio. It consists of 3200 acres and has fields with beans, potatoes, and other crops that are used to feed prisoners all across Ohio. There were several recreation areas, each with its own culture. The grass yard was for the readers and thinkers. The concrete yard was for us guys who "worked the iron pile," or "lifted weights" for you civilians. There was another yard that had two baseball diamonds encircled by a track. In addition to recreation, these areas were used for making deals and forming alliances.

After I was there a little bit, I was allowed to work the outside gang. After being locked up inside for so long, it was actually a bit of a treat! I'd get to work with rakes, shovels, work with silage, and work the vegetable fields. It really wasn't that bad. While I was there, I was in three different dormitories. I was in 7 Dorm when I started. Your dorm was classified according to your job. Dorms 1 and 7 were for the outside gang. 8 was for kitchen workers, and 5 Dorm housed custodial workers. I mention only those three because they were the three I was in.

I told you that fighting was the big thing for me. I had some experiences with the drugs and alcohol that we made, called hooch, and had been in trouble for getting tattoos, but my main problem area was fighting. I fought so much in 7 Dorm that they called me "Rocky of 7 Dorm." I wore that as a badge. Remember, I was just in my twenties. I even carried that persona with me when I got out. It worked for me. I didn't have to worry about anybody taking advantage of me.

Kenney the Knife King, a guy who slept next to me in 7 Dorm, was doing two fifteen to life sentences back to back. Fifteen to life meant nine years, six months before you got to go before the parole board. He was looking at a minimum of nineteen years. Kenney was not a very physical person like me, but he was very penitentiary smart. He was very good at the game. We formed a good working relationship once both of us realized that each of us had something the other lacked. I had physical prowess, and he had penitentiary savvy. If someone had something I wanted and they were weaker than me, I would just take it from them. I know it sounds cruel because it is. I'm just telling you like it is. I don't judge. People on the outside who get up, shave, and put on nice clothes everyday but still take from others are just as bad. My crimes have always been out on Front Street, not in the closet. I'd just tell you, "I want something, so I'm going to have it. It's up to you how I get it." Kenney was good at the game though. If you wanted something- a can of pop, a pack of cigarettes-he would get it for you, for a fee.

Most people survive on what the prison system gives you. I quit smoking because I couldn't afford cigarettes. The prison did supply us with Cardinal, which was free State tobacco, but it was horrible! It was so strong; it was like smoking chewing tobacco. People would rinse it just to try to take some of the edge off it. You could tell the people who smoked it because their mouths and fingers were horribly stained. Kenney kept a locker full of street stuff like hams, cheese, cookies, chips, pop, and cartons of cigarettes. He had so much of this stuff that he had other people storing it in their lockers too!

Kenney had a system in place that was not unlike those payday loan places on the outside, except he dealt in goods instead of money. You could get something from Kenney, but you would have to pay back with interest. Since the prison commissary was only open once a week, if you ran out of something in between you either waited or bought what you wanted from someone like Kenney. A common deal was to get one of something and promise to pay Kenney back with two of those same items when the commissary opened. This was called a "2 for 1." Come collection day, when maybe somebody didn't want to pay Kenney, that's where I came in. If they gave him a problem, he would send me to go collect from them what they owed-no more, no less. I got a portion of that. That's another thing I would carry with me when I left there-how to be a skilled collector, but more about that later.

There came a time when I just got tired of working the outside gang and wanted to be a dorm porter. The dorm porter's job was to sweep and mop. First, you had to move all the beds to one side of the room when the inmates got up to go to work. Then, you would sweep and mop, moving from dorm to dorm until all the floors were clean. That's all you'd do all day. When I was there, whites lived on one side, blacks on the other. The chow hall was the same, by inmate choice. There wasn't a whole lot of trouble that way.

I knew I had to play the game in order to get the dorm porter job. I had this knot on my leg from something I did in Xenia as a teen. I slipped on a rock when we were out rocking the winos. It didn't bother me at all, but I used it to go to the hospital so I could get reassigned to the porter job. They ended up putting me in 8 Dorm. When I got there, I began having a conversation with the guy in the bed next to mine. As soon as he found out where I was from, he said he used to live out there too. I slowly began to realize that I had read a story about this man in *Best True Fact Detective* while I was in the county jail.

This man I had just met told me about how he and another man had been involved in a drug deal. They decided they weren't going to give the dealer his money, so when the guy brought, the drugs they shot him. They then took a knife and cut out the bullets, put his body in a vehicle, and put it in long-term parking at an airport in Arizona. It didn't take long for the body to rot in that heat. They did a good job removing all traces of themselves until a couple years later, one of them was picked up in another state for selling drugs. To have the charges dropped, he told the authorities about the murder. That's how this man had been convicted. He was sent to a prison out in Arizona because that's where it happened. Through some type of prisoner exchange program, he ended up in a cell with me. Imagine yourself sleeping next to someone like that!

By that time, I was established as a predator. The story bothers me more now than it did then. At the time, I didn't give it a second thought. That's why Kenney the Knife King used me. He did his killing with a pistol, like the guy I just told you about. So, when it comes down to just what you're physically able to do with yourself, they needed me. Because I was a person who was never taught about right and wrong, only to do whatever a situation required, this arrangement suited me. I was needed. I knew I wasn't getting respect, but I *was* feared. I wanted to be feared as much then as I want to be respected now.

While I was in prison, my mom came once a month and gave me a twenty dollar bill. I would fold it up and put it in my bottom lip so that I could sneak it back through the strip down search that came after visitation and before going back into the prison. For those of you who don't know, cash is not allowed in prison. The only way inmates are supposed to buy anything is at the prison store, called a commissary, and to do that someone on the outside has to put money in a special account, or, *on the books*. The value of cash money in prison is that you can buy twice as much commissary items as you could with the same amount of money on the books.

Let me tell you how it works: Let's say a guy has marijuana smuggled in to the prison that has a $500 street value. He can sell that same amount of pot for $1250 cash, or $2500-worth of commissary items. Obviously, the guy is not going to want $2500-worth of Twinkies, so he converts it to cash by selling the commissary items for half price. That's where my twenty dollars in cash comes in. I can buy forty dollars-worth of commissary items from the pot guy for just twenty dollars, or half price. The guy will send his cash profit home through the mail. He's happy with a healthy 500% markup, and I'm happy with doubling my buying power.

Let me give you a picture of my relationship with my parents by that time. My parents were sober that one time a month, but they didn't see all the stuff that went on between the visits. You know, when you see someone just once a month, there's a lot that goes on that you miss. They saw me every month, but our connection wasn't close enough for them to know the THING that I was becoming. There was never any family counseling in the visitation rooms, it was, "Buy me some stuff out of the machines; some hot dogs and chips. Give me some money," and that was pretty much it. "See you again next month."

I'd like to know if my parents wanted things to be different, but they're both gone now. Even if they wanted things to be different, wanting things to be different and getting off your duff to make things happen are two different things. I don't know if there's any excuse for not trying. I know I was a handful, but why didn't they try harder? Looking at it from my point of view, I would have liked for things to be different, but I know I was a big project. As it turns out, I was a big project for God. God's authority is the only thing that has ever pierced my heart.

CHAPTER 10

His Reputation Preceded Him

While I was there in London, I heard about a man who would be coming to the prison. That man was Shorty Rat, president of the Dayton Outlaws at that time. Because of the reverence with which people referred to him, I was expecting a big, intimidating, mountain of a man. I pictured someone who was at least six foot four! I mean, he caused such a stir within the administration of the correctional institution that they pulled him aside right away and told him they didn't want any trouble from him. When he got to 7 Dorm, he got the best bed, the best TV location, and even locker boxes that had been filled with whatever he wanted before he even showed up! I compared my six foot one inch self who bench pressed 400 pounds on a daily basis to this five foot five inch guy. I thought to myself, "Really? People are steppin' and fetchin' for this man?" I was kind of ticked off, so I made a point to hang back from Shorty Rat. I knew Shorty Rat was untouchable because he had this posse that would follow him around. The respect he commanded was unnerving.

It wasn't long before prison life taught me something very important: Physical strength will only take you so far. Everything, even prison life, is a game of wits. I witnessed that men who were strong but not especially smart were often manipulated by the quick-witted. I had learned that those who were street-smart and intelligent can be more powerful than the man who is just physically strong.

One day, I was lying on my bed about half way up the row of metal bunks with my headphones on, listening to the radio. When I noticed Shorty Rat walking toward me, I quickly decided not to say anything to him. He stopped at the foot of my bunk, obviously aware that I had headphones on- yet he just stood there waiting like he knew I'd take them off to see what he had to say. He tapped the end of my bed. Just a few seconds went by, but it seemed like a long time. I reached up and took the headphones off. All he said was, "Let's take a walk, Shooter." You could tell he was used to talking to people like me a certain way. I felt good that the president of the Dayton Outlaws was talking to me, but knew I needed to get past his exterior.

That exchange taught me something about myself. I realized that I had fallen right in line like everybody else. At Shorty Rat's beckoning, I had gotten right up out of bed and followed him onto the yard. At the time I thought that all we did that day was walk laps, but with the perspective that comes from years and experience, I know he was schooling me. He was letting me know that he saw some abilities I had, but that he didn't *need* me. I gained more respect among the inmates that afternoon, just walking the track with Shorty Rat, than I had gotten from all the years of fighting. While we were walking, he told me that he wanted me to get in touch with some people he knew when I got released. What I took away from that more than anything was the message, "I know some people that will love you, accept you, and understand you just the way you are." I think people would be lying if they said they weren't looking for something like that. It was a very important day in my life. He never made me any promises, and he never asked me for anything. I realized for myself why people talked about Shorty Rat the way they did. I understood it all: he made them feel good about themselves. He made them feel that they were human beings, not just animals shoved into a cage, given a number and forgotten about. He made me believe there was a group of people on the outside who would love and accept me. That's a powerful message, no matter who it comes from. The feeling is the same if you believe it.

Today I have that same feeling about Jesus Christ, but as a twenty-something kid, I was just beginning to figure out that nobody was coming to help me. Superman wasn't going to swoop in and save me. Batman wasn't coming with his tool belt. The Green Lantern wasn't coming with his magic ring. Up until the moment I met Jesus, I just knew it was me against the world.

I ran into Shorty Rat after I got out. I didn't join the Outlaws, but I joined another motorcycle club called the Riders. One day, we got word that Shorty Rat was getting out of prison, and I made sure to mention that I had been in prison with him. Other people let on that they were friends of his, too. Shorty Rat was a big deal in that community, so a big party at the Hot Rock on Main Street in Dayton was planned. When we all showed up at the Hot Rock that night, I saw that, just like in prison, he had drawn a crowd and the place was just packed with people from a variety of clubs. These were people who were supporting him and giving him gifts. I knew why they treated him that way in a way I didn't really understand the first time he came to 7 Dorm back in London Correctional.

When he emerged from the back room, everybody went crazy over him, stepping up to be recognized by The King. I was standing in the back, drinking my beer when he saw me across the room and made a B-line through all those people who were salivating over his presence. He walked right up to *me*, gave *me* a big brotherly hug, and asked *me* how I was doing. I had instant credibility in the motorcycle community.

When I was finally paroled and released, I carried out with me the attitude that the world owed me something. It was the world's fault that it had come against me. I was pretty much state-raised from the age of twelve. My foundation was parents who did not teach me right from wrong, and things just progressively got worse from there. I had experienced foster homes, juvenile lock up, and penitentiaries. My mentality was that you just dealt with each situation the best you knew how. Consequences were not part of the equation. Healthy people factor consequences into the equation when they are thinking something through. That wasn't a part of me at twenty-five years old. I don't believe that it was my fault, I just had never been shown any other way.

Yes, we are each responsible for our actions. But at twenty-five, I thought I had taken the consequences for my actions. I thought, "I've done my prison time; now, get out of my face." The way I was raised, things are either black or white; there aren't many gray areas in life. As demanding of myself as I was back then, I'm still demanding when it comes to my spiritual life. I believe that you're either a servant of Jesus Christ or you're not. You either believe, or you don't. You either trust him, or you don't.

CHAPTER 11

Paroled/Riders

When I was paroled, I was thrust back into a home life that really didn't make sense. I was once small and weak like the rest of the people at home. I went to prison a small, weak person and came out big, strong, and used to survival of the fittest. I was an evolutionist's dream. After I accepted Jesus Christ into my heart, I realized that life is not all about survival of the fittest. Life is about everyone, not just the strong, having the opportunity to have life and to have it more abundantly. My parents said I could stay with them until I got on my feet, but that lasted just a matter of weeks.

When I got out of prison, I not only started a relationship with the woman who would become my first wife, I joined the Riders. I worked during this time, but my real motivation was to be a respected member of the club. Those were the people that I had been told on the prison yard would love me and accept me with all my faults. As a matter of fact, they wouldn't see any faults. They were honest and up front. They didn't hide when they did drugs. They didn't think one thing and say something else. I was in the club for six or eight months when I was asked to move up to Enforcer. S'cuse was moving up from the role of Enforcer, so they needed someone to take over. I finally arrived where I was supposed to be in life! Of course, I accepted the job. If we had a party at the clubhouse, I was the security guy. If there were any problems, I was expected to take care of them, whether inside or around the clubhouse. If you'd never been there before, I was the person who would read you the rules. If you broke a rule, I'd be the one who would come see you and have a *talk* with the person who brought you.

These days, when I try to explain to people what I did as Enforcer, I explain it like this: I was the guy who showed up at your house after the talking was done. I would tell people who'd try to talk to me when I showed up, "You should have talked to the last guy who was here." In other words, by the time I was called in to handle a matter, negotiations had failed and it was time to take it to a different level.

We used to go out to a place called Sinking Springs for our breakout run. A breakout run is when the entire club gets together for a ride and a party after a long, cold winter. It was a big event, and usually there would be one or two other clubs that would go with us. It was a place far enough away from civilization that we could pretty much do whatever we wanted without fear of the police coming in and shutting us down. We'd shoot our guns. We'd get drunk. As Enforcer, I was in charge of that event so that our president could have some R&R.

If a patch holder (club member) got in trouble for something, I was the one who was sent to take care of that also. Sometimes it meant giving the guy a probate patch (demotion), sometimes it meant taking his colors (club affiliation patch). Sometimes it meant more.

My relationship with the club came to a dramatic end when I quit the Riders in 1996. I've been back to the clubhouse since then, but my last night there as a Rider, I had already been drinking and was in a foul mood. Ogre and I were on our way to *church*, which is what we called our club meetings, when he asked, "Why don't I just drop you off here at the Santa Fe?" He figured things wouldn't go well if I went to the meeting. I agreed and he went on to the meeting. Soon after entering the bar, some guy started some trouble with me. During all my time in the club I had never dropped a dime on anybody; I had never made a phone call to summon reinforcements to come help me deal with a situation. Tonight would be different. I made my way over to the pay phone, called the clubhouse and told them I was having some problems at the Santa Fe. I went back over and sat on the barstool to wait. Within fifteen minutes, there were twenty Riders coming in both the front and back doors. For years as Enforcer, I had been the one summoned to help with other people's problems. It was cool sitting there watching other people handle a situation.

We all got into vehicles and went back to the clubhouse. Probably about half the people were high fiving, saying things like, "We stick up for each other! We're a brotherhood," but there was this other faction that thought I messed up. They told me, "You're too crazy, always shooting your guns. People from other clubs don't want to come around because of you." This brotherhood that I was promised was going to love and protect me was *against* me. It was all a big lie. Though I was in a room of at least twenty people, I instantly felt alone among them. It just didn't go well. I remember somebody hollering at Danno, the president, to grab me. Danno said, "You grab him. That's why I'm president, I know better than to grab him." He walked me out, saying, "Don't worry, everybody's been drinking," trying to console me or something. I told him, "No, it's over."

Now that I no longer had my club family, I found myself thinking back in time. I thought back to my childhood in Sarasota so long ago when I was just a little boy playing in the sunshine. Because I was just a youngster, I didn't know that my parents didn't have any money. I remembered the happy times before the alcohol, drugs, violence, and infidelity completely ravaged our family. Once my family fell apart, my sense of belonging fell apart, too. Like any other kid I just wanted to belong to something, so I tried to find that sense of belonging in other places. I remembered wanting to be on the football team, trying out and making it but being told I couldn't be on the team because I didn't look right. I remembered all the years in prison, cut off from normal society. Even the motorcycle club would not be the family that I wanted and needed so much. And now, here again, what I heard was, "You don't belong."

Things really started coming to a head pretty quickly after that last night in the clubhouse. While I was in the club, I had been collecting money for a guy called Fifth Street Bill. When people wouldn't pay their debts, Fifth Street Bill would send me to take care of it, and I'd get a percentage of what I collected. People thought he had a cool 'street' name. Actually, he got the name for more practical reasons: he lived on 5th Street and his first name was Bill. I had done time with him-he was a big drug dealer who also ran a poker game.

I was over at his house partying one night, not talking about business at all, when Fifth Street Bill said, "I don't want you collecting for me anymore."

"Why not?" I asked, "I thought I did a pretty good job for you."

"You do," he answered. "That's the problem. The word on the street is that people don't want to take a beating from you. If they see you coming, they're gonna put a bullet in you. Man, I love you. You can do drugs, sell drugs, or whatever you want. I don't want you getting killed working for me." I know he was just trying to look out for me, but all I could think about was the large percentage of income that had just dried up—right before my eyes.

This is about the time when I made that unannounced stop at Greg's old farm house in the country and contemplated killing him. I'm sure that just losing a source of income contributed to the thoughts I had of putting a bullet into Greg that night. It's not that I was angry at Greg, it's just that by this time I operated from a purely animalistic level. He had something I wanted and I was going to take it. That's how it works for a predator and its prey.

I didn't act on those thoughts. We did our deal, and I went on my way. About thirty days later, I got a call from Greg's girlfriend.

She and Greg had been fighting, and she had gone to stay with her mom. A few days later, someone called and asked her to check on the apartment because there was a foul smell coming from the place. When she went to check the apartment, she found Greg. He was dead, sitting on the couch with the dope on the table and the needle still stuck in his arm.

I thought about all the messages I had left on Greg's answering machine since that night in his house. I had left several messages asking when another shipment was going to come in. I imagined the sound of me leaving messages for Greg on his answering machine while he was sitting there, already dead on his couch.

Greg's girlfriend called me again later, asking if I would give the eulogy at his funeral. She explained that they were going to bury him at a really nice spot out in the country, somewhere Greg would have liked. She wanted me say a few kind words because I was the only friend he had. Of course, I told her I'd do it. I think everybody should have somebody say something over them. Don't get me wrong; Greg was a nice guy. He made bad decisions, and unfortunately, one of those decisions cost him his life. I remember the day of the funeral, the closed casket, the gorgeous spot, and the smiling faces of the family members as I prepared to speak. My struggle that day was the realization that I was standing over this man's casket saying all these wonderful things about him, knowing that just a month before I had been thinking about putting a bullet in him.

I had finally turned the spotlight on myself and realized that I was a sick man. If something didn't change drastically, I was going to wind up just like Greg: dead with someone trying to find one friend who would say nice things over my casket.

CHAPTER 12

I Have a Drug Problem

Just a handful of weeks after that, I was doing my drug of choice, crystal meth, when I got into an argument with my wife about my dependency on it. I told her that I was addicted to it and had no control over it. She said that I just used my addiction to the drug as an excuse to keep using it. As the argument intensified, I got a phone book out to prove my point. I found a drug hotline, called the number and talked to a guy named Rodney out in California. I talked to him for a while, and he agreed with me. He said that I had no control over my addiction. I asked him to tell my wife that, so I put her on the phone, and he did. I got back on and was ready to hang up, since my point had been made, but he said, "Hold on now. We need to talk about recovery."

He talked me into admitting myself in a treatment center the next morning at 8 a.m., but I warned him that if I was coming down from a high or sober by then, I wouldn't care what I was booked into. I just wouldn't go. I'll never forget his words, "Go get some more. We don't care if you show up high. We'll deal with that when you get here. If you need to go to your buddy's and get more to last you, go do it." I realized that I had been talking to someone who had lived in my shoes. I made it through the night, and by 8 a.m. I was at the drug treatment center in Toledo, Ohio. Right away, I just laid it on the line, and they were very supportive. I called my boss and he assured me that my job would be there when I got back. Things were really lining up for me! I believed things were finally going to get better.

About two weeks into treatment, though, a woman came in from AA. She said, "Statistically, one of you will not pick up again. Out of twenty men, only one will never use alcohol or drugs again." What a disappointment! I had gone there expecting to be fixed, either by therapy or medication. As usual, I was looking for a quick fix. I didn't realize that it would take years to undo what had taken years to build.

Alone in my room that night, I sat on my bed thinking about my entire life, and something started to develop inside me. It was unfamiliar, almost foreign. I felt something coming from a place inside of me that I didn't know was there. I know now that this was the indwelling of the Holy Spirit. Scripture tells us that when God creates us, he instills a measure of faith so we'll have that when we make the decision to cry out to Him. I used that measure of faith that night. I saw myself as a little boy, running across the front yard to the church bus just as fast as I could. Nice people were on the church bus. I remembered going down into the basement classroom into the church, looking at a picture of Jesus surrounded by children, and wanting to be one of those children so badly.

I can only describe what happened to me like this: It's like digging a hole on the beach right by the water. There's no water in that hole to begin with, but when you scoop out a trench, all of a sudden the hole is filled with water. Before I realized it, I was on my knees weeping. I don't remember crying from the moment that my dad shot that man until this moment. Crying was for the weak. I couldn't be weak; I was on my own. I hadn't cried for twenty-six years.

On my knees in the dark, I had a conversation with God. I talked to God. He knew what I'd been through, and with all His grace and mercy, He came to where I was. I realized that He had been there all along. I learned something very important about God that night. First, I learned that He will come to you no matter where you are. He knew exactly what I needed that night. He knew I needed His Son, Jesus Christ. I talked to God and told Him, "I don't know how to do this. I've heard a lot about this, but I don't know what hoop to jump through or fancy words to say." The second thing I learned about God is that He doesn't care about fancy. He doesn't care what house you live in, what car you drive, or how long your hair is. What He does care about is your faith and trust in Him. Here's what I heard in my heart that night from God. "Believe in my Son, trust Him, and I will prove to you that I am in charge." Those are words I understood, and I accepted His offer.

Right away, I could feel that there was something different about me. I once heard it explained in a sermon this way, "Why wouldn't you feel different after the Holy Spirit has moved into your body? Wouldn't you know it if somebody moved into your house? There's crumbs on the counter; somebody sitting in your chair watching TV." For the first time in my life, I felt good inside.

Me (front), my brother Timmy, Mom, and the Harley Davidson. This is the bike my dad rode Mom to the hospital on when she was in labor with me.

(front to back) Stormy the Goat, Timmy, age 7 and my sister Lisa, age 2, me at age 6.

Christmas 1971, about a year before my dad shot the neighbor. (front to back) Lisa, age 6, Timmy and me, ages 10 and 11, Dad and Mom, ages 33 and 29.

My dad with one of our horses, before he went to prison and we lost everything.

Me, age 16, at Buckeye Youth Center doing my first real time.

*Me and my dad on Visiting Day at London
Correctional Institution 1983.*

*(left to right) My dad, uncle, and me with my
1950 Panhead in my dad's front yard.*

*Riders MC Breakout Run. Sinking Springs,
Ohio, 1996. (left to right) Cocheese, Ogre, me, and
Dano [Riders MC President at the time].*

Knowing Jesus–before and after. On the left, me in the 1990s. On the right, me as I appear today.

Riders MC 26-Year Reunion. Riders Clubhouse, Dayton, Ohio, 2014. Members and friends (left to right) Mad Max, Tramp, Ogre, Breeze, Shooter [me], Big Daddy, Chucky, Singe, Dan, TBone, and Opossum.

How it All Changed: A New Creation

CHAPTER 13

A New Beginning

After the treatment center, I went back to my house and my job. Right away, I felt drawn to read the Bible. I found a Bible around the house somewhere and opened it up. I went right to the red letters. I wasn't completely ignorant. I knew the red letters were Jesus' words. I knew that all the words were inspired by God, but the red words were actually spoken by Jesus when he was alive on this earth. I could understand what the words said, but no revelations came.

You see, God had a plan for me, and His plan for me was not to sit in my room and read the Bible. I said my second prayer in my walk with the Lord. I asked Him to give me someone who would help me understand His Word. He knew the kind of assistance that I needed, so He sent me to one of His soldiers. This soldier happened to live next door and is named Don Baughn. I had lived there for five years and never spoken to the man or his wife before. I found out later that they had been continually praying for me and my situation.

Those are the kind of people God knew I needed in my life. The next day, I was standing at the fence talking with Don. At that time, I knew nothing about their prayers or their walk with the Lord. I was just standing at the fence having a friendly conversation about the weather or something when I felt compelled to tell him about what had happened to me that night in the treatment center. He just took it in, without much of expression on his face to give me any read on his reaction. He said things like, "Really? That's interesting." When

I finally took a breath, he said, "Hey, why don't you come over for coffee?" I did, and he put on a pot of coffee, opened a pack of cookies, and we sat down. It's fifteen years later, and it's been many cups of coffee and countless packs of cookies since we began our walk together. I've spent countless hours sitting with Don and his wife Wanda at their kitchen table, poring over God's Word.

Don has shared things with me that only a seasoned veteran of God can know. I remember the little smile on Don's face when he said, "I want you to remember this." He had this old cracked Bible that was full of notes, highlighter marks, and bookmarks shoved between the pages. It was as if this book was an extension of himself. He put his hand on the Bible, almost caressing it. He said, "Don't ever believe anything that comes out of my mouth unless I can back it up with God's Word."

I followed Don Baughn around everywhere. He took me to a Bible study at one church and to another church for a service. It was at the little stone church on Huffman Avenue in Dayton, Ohio that I answered a formal altar call, speaking the words with my mouth and surrendering my life to Jesus Christ. It wasn't too long after that-- maybe a couple of months into this--that Don called me up and said, "I was reading the paper and I saw that Mark Brooks is starting a new church. I think we need to go." So, we went to the first service of A House Of Prayer, called AHOP for short, in Xenia, Ohio. That night they did a moving dramatization of what I now know was the Passion of Christ. For the first time in my life, I heard a preacher speak openly about his past broken marriage, alcoholism, and the bondage of sin. He explained that Jesus is the way, the truth, and the life. These were incredible, earth-shattering ideas! I thought, "Wow, this preacher has been through things just like I have." I knew I needed to go back. Well, I kept going back to that church for the next seven or eight years.

CHAPTER 14

Malachi 3:3

In all those years I spent at A House Of Prayer, there were times I wanted to give up, that I wanted to quit. You know, during that time I had to deal with the fallout of the way I had been living. My marriage was part of the fallout, and it didn't survive. Yes, even though I was making better lifestyle decisions, some of the transition was painful. I could only hope that there would be some purpose for this pain. My answer came from the Book of Malachi. "He will sit as a refiner and a purifier of silver; He will purify the sons of Levi, and purge them as gold and silver, that they may offer to the Lord an offering in righteousness" Malachi 3:3 (NKJV).

I've heard the Scripture explained like this: Inspired by Malachi 3:3, a woman went to a silversmith to learn more about the refining process. She arrived and noticed that the first thing the silversmith did was attach a piece of rock to the end of a metal rod. She asked him, "Where's the silver?"

He replied, "It's inside the rock. It's my job to get it out." His next step was to take this piece of rock that he had attached to the rod and stick it into a flame. She watched him very carefully as he didn't just hold the rock in one place, but he'd move it into the fire, pull it back a little, then move it back into the fire.

Her next question was, "Why do you keep moving it in and out of the fire?"

"Because I don't want to burn the silver up. I am trying to burn the impurities out of it and leave the silver."

Her final question was, "How do you know when you're done?"

He smiled and replied, "That's easy: When I can see my reflection in it."

I know that while I am here on this earth, I will always be in a stage somewhere between rock and silver. I have learned that the process of purification that God puts us through can be excruciating at times, but it has a purpose. I remember one time it was so painful that I thought, "God, I can't take it anymore."

His reply was, "I know it's uncomfortable but you said you would trust in Me."

I said, "Why are you doing this?"

He replied, "Because I want you to be like Jesus."

I answered, "But He's your Son."

Then God said, "You still don't get it, Doug, so are you."

Eventually, AHOP had an opportunity to buy the American Legion building in Xenia. AHOP doesn't take a traditional offering. Instead, there were boxes places at the exits of the building. You can put your donations there. Since this was a special situation, Pastor Mark told the congregation that in one month's time there would be a special offering taken up during the service to raise money for the purchase of the Legion Hall. I went to my boss, who was a good Christian man, and told him about what AHOP was trying to do. I was in no position to give a donation that would amount to anything at that time, unless I could get overtime. My boss agreed, and I must have worked seventy hours that week.

Payday came, and I got this big fat check, which I took home and prayed over. I really wanted to open the communication lines with God. "How much of this do you want me to give?"

I instantly heard His response. "All of it."

I said, "You want me to what? I can't give all of it. I have $35 to make it through next week. I need gas and groceries."

Again speaking in a way I can understand, He said, "Why'd you ask me if you're not going to listen? Give it all." He always takes me back to that room in the drug treatment center when He told me that He would prove to me that he was in charge. So, I agreed to give it all.

I wanted to use this as an example of pure obedience to my son, so I collected him up and took him to meet with Pastor Mark. Neither Pastor Mark nor my son knew why we were there. As my sixteen year-old listened, I told the story about how God told me to give it all. I took the check out of my pocket and said, "You got a pen?" Tears started to well up in Pastor Mark's eyes. Not because I was about to sign over a check, but because he was witnessing the glory of God shining through this ex-convict and drug addict. I signed the check over and handed it to him, and he just sat there and wept. All three of us were blubbering in his office when Pastor Mark's wife, Anna, came in and said, "What's going on?" She ended up crying right along with us.

For the next week, I lived on 69-cent TV dinners. The Lord provided, as He always does. A month after that, I got word from the boss that the powers that be wanted me to work second shift. I turned them down. He said, "But you'd be boss."

I said, "I'll tell you what. Tell them I want x amount of money." I was trying to counter in such a way that they would deny me. To my surprise, they met my terms! The raise I got was exactly one hundred fold what I gave to Pastor Mark over a year's time. Just another example that God is in charge. He's in control. All we have to do is believe, walk in obedience, and have faith that He will provide. In fact, in His timing, He saw fit to provide me with a second chance at marriage.

My wife, Tanya, and I attended the same church for seven years before actually speaking to each other. Our sons got involved with something together in the church, and that led to me asking her out for coffee. While we were having coffee, I gave her my number-- just in case her son needed to contact my son, of course.

The truth is I couldn't wait for her to call me. I remember lying in bed that night watching TV and checking my phone repeatedly to make sure I hadn't missed her call. I finally fell asleep still holding the phone in my hand. Luckily, she called not long after I fell asleep.

We talked for hours. We shared deeply about ourselves right away and realized that we connected on many levels. We talked some about how life had beat us both up some before we finally gave in to the tug on our hearts by Jesus. We talked about things like the tough lessons learned and about our hopes and dreams. It wasn't long before we knew that we wanted to build a relationship, but resolved not to base it on past pain or negativity of any kind. We knew that if we acknowledged our past hurts and pains but did not define ourselves by them, we could build a relationship on the strengths that each of us had to offer. In other words, it was important to both of us to build a relationship on our mutual love of Christ and see where it would lead. From the very beginning, we knew that we had to make God the center of everything in our relationship if it was going to work. We knew that dealing with the fallout from past relationships and becoming a blended family would be tough, but if we let God lead us it would be a successful marriage.

Our first date with the kids was at Kings Island. I'll never forget the first time we were on top of the Eiffel Tower. There was not one cloud in the sky, and we could see for miles. As we stood side by side gazing into the distance, I noticed that I could see Lebanon Correctional Institution's recreation yard. Without thinking, I blurted, "Hey look, you can see one of the prisons I was in from here!" You can imagine the looks from her and the other thirty people up there-they were priceless. Typical of Tanya's understated nature, she commented, "Oh, that's nice," the same way she would have if I had been pointing out any other part of the landscape. At that moment, I knew that she had a heart of acceptance and not of condemnation.

Our life together has been filled with events like that, and I feel incredibly blessed. Over the years, God has used her in my recovery from emotional wounds that never seemed to heal. She is a patient listener and gentle guide. She's everything I'm not. I am big and loud, she is petite and quiet. I love working with my hands, she loves reading and writing. I like to be "out front," whereas she likes to work behind the scenes. She has a quiet strength that balances my intensity. We like to say that we are complementary, or as Rocky said, "We fill each other's gaps." We are such a good team, and I could fill another book with all the things that are right about our relationship.

The first time my wife asked me about my experiences moving from poverty to middle class, I didn't even realize I was middle class. I make jokes that when I was growing up, we were so poor that we fought over the little piece of fat in the can of pork and beans, but we really weren't. For the first eleven years of my life, my dad was a hard worker and had a good job at a department store called Moss Brothers. My dad always had some kind of Harley Davidson. My mom would plan meals for the week and cook us supper. I remember getting a brand new bicycle for my birthday one year and watching my dad put it together. I would ride it down to one of those mom and pop stores to get a big slab of green apple gum for a nickel. I think we were in what is called the working class, until my dad shot that man. I believe that people can be raised in a decent environment no matter how much money they have. Unfortunately, my home environment included domestic violence and alcoholism.

After the shooting, we did live in poverty, and I'm sure that had an effect on me. Before my dad shot that man, we had lived in a place where we kids could run around and play outside. After my dad went to prison, all that disappeared. Life was my mom trying to take care of three kids, all of us living in a rented room in a boarding house where the only bathroom was shared with everybody on the floor. We had few clothes and had to look for food. My mom spent her time trying to get help from the state and hoping one of the succession of men she brought into her life would provide something. I didn't understand what was happening to our family, but I definitely *felt* the difference between working class and poverty.

Once in a while, someone will ask me how I was able to move into the middle class. I tell them, "If you don't like where you are in life, find someone who is where you want to be and start doing more of what they do." In other words, find a model or a mentor; expand your knowledge. I've already mentioned two of the godly men in my life who filled that role for me: Don Baughn and Pastor Mark Brooks. Two others have been Pastor Bruce Craig and Pastor David Smith.

I first noticed Pastor Bruce Craig's intense desire to take me closer to Jesus during a class for new attendees at his church. He looked at my wife and me and asked us to share our definition of grace. This is hard for me to admit, but after all the years I had been a Christ follower up to that point, which was years, I stumbled around with finding an answer to that question. He let us wrestle with it for a little while before he stepped in and said, "Grace is God's unmerited favor for you. He favors you so much that He sent his only Son to die for you on the cross." He taught us about all kinds of grace. That was our first of many faith-deepening encounters with Pastor Bruce Craig.

From then on, it just got better and better. His messages were direct and to the point. He was too bold for some, unfortunately, but it was what I personally needed for that season of my life. Pastor Bruce Craig is one of the most humble men I've ever had the pleasure of knowing. From the pulpit, you see and feel his boldness. He is aggressive about God's Word, about His plan for us, and about *what is not God's plan* for us. Though he is a ball of fire when he preaches, he is the humblest of men when you sit and talk to him for council. I believe that Pastor Bruce feels honored to have been chosen by God to preach His Word and to be a pastor. He lives his calling not just at church, but twenty-four/seven, every day of the week. In all the years I've known Pastor Bruce, I've never caught him off point from the directive that God has given him. His confidence in me, his brothers and sisters, and others is astounding. He chooses to see the good in people, because that's God's plan for all of us.

It's hard to sum up Pastor David Smith in just a few words, but I will tell you about my first encounter with him as a way to illustrate the kind of man he is: My wife, my daughter, and I had been going to Fairhaven for just a few weeks, when I had an opportunity to speak to Pastor Smith in the foyer after a service. Making small talk, I learned that he had once been a motorcycle rider and had interest in getting another bike someday. By this time, I had spoken at several Biker

Sundays and started Forged By Fire, and I had big plans. Somewhere in the conversation, I asked, "You know what I see, Pastor Smith?"

Smiling, he responded, "No, Doug, why don't you tell me?"

I put my arm around his shoulder, turned him around to face the parking lot and said, "I see that parking lot full of motorcycles."

Continuing to smile, he said two things: "Let's make that happen," and "How can I help?"

That's quite a response, especially considering that Pastor Smith has a flock of over four thousand people! Pastor Smith is many things, including a great teacher, father, husband, and Christ-follower, but nothing speaks louder than his heart to serve. Asking, "How can I help?" that day spoke volumes about Pastor's Smith's character, an attitude of humility that he has consistently demonstrated for all the years I have known him.

Allowing others to mentor me led me to follow through with making changes in my life. I have learned that improving your life is really a matter of common sense when you boil it down. I recommend choosing just a couple of things to change at one time. For example, maybe your chosen model has quit smoking and uses the savings to fund an annual vacation. You might decide to do the same. Result: You are improving your health and taking a fun trip every year! You've just moved yourself up a notch.

Another element to improving your life is letting go of unforgiveness. Holding onto bitterness and resentment toward others holds you back. I once heard a sermon about forgiveness that taught me something very important: Forgiveness doesn't require reconciliation. In other words, you can forgive someone but still maintain distance from them. Understanding the nature of forgiveness released me from the guilt and shame connected to past hurts, allowing me to move forward with God's plan for my life.

Small steps can lead you to the life you want to have. This is very important: You must believe that change is possible in order to be successful! You must shed the mindset that you are limited to the world that you may have grown up in. It's about opening your heart so He can make you, me, us-overcomers. It's about believing "I can do anything through Christ who strengthens me." (Philippians 4:13, NKJV). For me, it all started with giving my life to Christ. All of the positive changes in my life are due to His help. God wants you to be healthy and to experience joy. You can be an overcomer with the strength that comes from Him!

New Things Have Come

CHAPTER 15

Forged By Fire

As I said, when you give your life to Christ, He will help you overcome things that you never thought you could. The Bible says, "You have not because you ask not. (James 4:2, NKJV). My wife and I take to heart the words, "I have come that they might have life, and that they may have it more abundantly." (John 10:10 NKJV). Abundance can come in many ways. As Christians, there is nothing wrong with wanting abundance. For example, we wanted a nicer home, more reliable vehicles, for our daughter to go to a better school. We wanted to share out of our abundance to reach others. It is through that desire to share God's abundance that I began to feel drawn to use my motorcycle to reach others.

Ever since my dad bought me my first bike from Hap's Harley Davidson in Sarasota, FL when I was ten years old, I've ridden a motorcycle (except for the times I've been a guest of the State of Ohio, of course). I felt such joy when I realized that God was not going to take that away from me, but instead, He would use it for His purpose. People have the misconception that once they become a believer, God will lead them to stop everything they have ever enjoyed doing in their life. This is a lie. God will purposely leave things in your life but turn them in such a way that they work for good and glorify Him. It's true that motorcycle riding had been intertwined with all the bad things that I was doing in my life, but at some point I realized that I actually enjoyed the act of riding itself. This realization came once He took all the bad stuff away, and I was just left with God, the motorcycle, and the open road.

I believe that God could remove all memory of our lives before being saved, but what good would it do? We wouldn't be able to talk to someone who's sitting there with a needle in his arm, and tell him, "You know, you don't have to do that." Nothing in a needle ever gave me the feeling that I have all day long with Him. After my wife and I prayed about it, the decision was made to start a motorcycle ministry.

I designed our insignia, which is an anvil with two crossed swords going into it. The anvil signifies substance. I've seen anvils that were 150 years old and looked just the same as the day they were made. The anvil was made to change the shape of metal, so you can take a piece of steel, heat it up, put it on the anvil and reshape it, but the anvil itself is unchanging, like God. It has weight and substance, like God. God can take us no matter what kind of crazy shape we're in and shape us to His liking. The swords represent God's Word. My wife came up with the name Forged By Fire, and we chose Malachi 3:3 to go along with the logo. We then go to work on our *colors*, the club patch that is worn on the back of a member's jacket. After we put our colors together, we started working on writing up a statement of what we believe.

Next, we sat down and tossed around ideas of how to introduce Forged By Fire to the community. Looking back, I can see how God blessed our desire to serve right away by leading us to Paul and Nan Zanowick. At the time, they were facing the one-year anniversary of the death of their son, CPL Paul "Rocky" Zanowick II. Rocky was a Marine who was killed by a sniper in Afghanistan on June 3, 2011. Paul and Nan shared at our first meeting that at the age of 15, Rocky decided to enlist in the Marine Corps after seeing the horror of airplanes intentionally crashed into American buildings. They talked about feeling a strong need to commemorate the anniversary of their son's death in some way, but were not yet sure *how*.

At that moment, I knew that Forged By Fire was meant to make that happen for the Zanowicks. Over the next few weeks, we worked together to plan and host a memorial program and tribute ride to honor their son, both of which were well attended by the military and civilian communities. Rocky's parents gave me one of the memorial coins they had made. The coin has a picture of Rocky on it, and it is displayed proudly on my leather vest. Even though I never met Rocky in life, I know that he is loved and missed very much and I look forward to meeting him in heaven one day.

Armed with a vision and passion for Forged By Fire Motorcycle Ministry, God has provided opportunities for me to speak in many venues- from prisons and churches to high schools filled with troubled teens who are dealing with the same crap I was dealing with at their age. As someone with the motorcycle background that I have, I felt excited that God's plan for me involved my bike. In the beginning, I believed that Forged By Fire would be an instrument of God to witness to the motorcycle community. As usual in my relationship with God, He had a different plan. Forged By Fire is involved with things in the motorcycle community such as biker Sundays and bike nights, but the Lord has opened up two very unexpected but rewarding doors for us.

CHAPTER 16

Prison Ministry

O ne of those doors is prison ministry. My first experience with prison ministry was with Chuck Colson's Prison Fellowship Ministry. A friend of mine who knew some of my story called me up and asked if this was something I might be interested in. I told him I would pray about it and get back with him. With the feelings I had of walking back into prison, I wanted to make sure that this was really part of God's plan for me. After lots of prayer, I felt God giving me the green light. After all the forms were filed, I was approved to be a part of Prison Fellowship Ministry.

At that point, I had no idea what prison I would visit first. I remember getting the call from my friend and being told that my first visit would be in Orient, Ohio. I remember my friend's disbelief when I told him that out of the five prisons I had been locked up in, Orient was the last one. Unbelievable that God had planned that the first prison I would go into to minister was the last prison I had walked into as an inmate! I accepted, but as the date drew closer, I found myself reliving all the years that I spent locked up behind bars. As I was doing that, I kept hearing in my heart, "Tell them how you overcame all of this. Give them hope. Let them know that this doesn't have to be their legacy. Make them understand that through Jesus Christ they can become good fathers and good husbands. Tell them that they can have joy in their life."

As I prepared for my first visit to prison as a Christ follower, I started to realize the responsibility that comes with being a Christian. I had realized that salvation is just the beginning. There are a lot of words you could put in this statement, "With _____, comes great responsibility." I say, "With *salvation* comes great responsibility. At that moment in my life, that was what God was teaching me.

I will never forget that day. On the trip up, sitting in the back seat of the car, my thoughts went back to a similar trip I had taken so many years before, when I sat alone in the back seat of the sheriff's car with two sheriffs in the front seat. My friend and his brother were in the front seat this time, but I felt every bit like the nervous eighteen-year-old I had been on my first ride to prison facing fifteen years of incarceration.

My senses were just as alive that day as they had been so many years earlier. The difference was that, instead of being alive with thoughts of dread and fear of the unknown, this time my senses were alive with the things of the Spirit. God told me, "Through Jesus Christ you are an overcomer. On your first trip, you knew you were on your way to a battlefield. Today, you are on the way to a battlefield, too. The difference is that you are not going to physical battle. Today, you are going to a spiritual battle."

Those messages changed my perspective on that day and every day I have spent inside a prison ever since. I wasn't going back in there as an ex-convict to tell them how to deal with life as an inmate, I was there for a much greater purpose. I was there to help by showing them something tangible-something they could put their hands on-an example of what Christ can do when you trust in Him.

We got there about five minutes late. I remember the looks of the inmates that day as we walked into the room. There were about eighty of them. We found our way to the back and quietly took our seats, not wanting to disturb the session that was already in progress. As the chaplain was explaining the steps to salvation, I could *feel* the inmates staring at me. I didn't understand how obvious it was to them that I had once been an inmate just like them until later on when we broke into small groups for discussion. "We knew you were one of us when you walked through the door," they told me. Because I was once in the same place as those inmates, I had credibility with them. I haven't been in a prison since then where I haven't instantly gotten credibility because I have been "one of them" and come back.

While speaking at a church in Ohio recently, I shared a story about something that happened to me while at a prison in Indiana with Bill Glass Ministries. I had been instantly attracted to his ministry because participating meant that I would get to ride my motorcycle inside the prison. Just like my past as an inmate, my motorcycle is a tool I use to break the ice. Some of the men come out onto the yard during these events just because they want to come out and see the motorcycles, and that's okay with me, because it gives me a chance to talk about what Jesus has done for me.

During the second session, while a lady was singing on stage, I scanned the group of men, sensing that they were somehow different from the first group of inmates I had talked to that morning. The ability to read people that was part of my survival in prison serves me to this day. Sometimes I wonder if people who haven't had to survive on their wits have the same level of sensitivity about reading people. While speaking to one of the inmates, it came to light that this group of inmates was from the PC unit. These are the inmates that you hear are locked down in protective custody, separated from the other inmates so they can't hurt them. These are people like child molesters and rapists. For those of you who don't know, in the prison culture there is a class structure, and sex offenders are at the bottom.

I'm going to be as transparent as I can be: I did not want to minister to these men. Standing in this prison yard in Indiana, all I could think about were the horrible things they must have done to be there. I spoke to the Lord, saying, "God, I don't feel comfortable doing this." And here's what I heard back: "Doug, my Son wasn't comfortable hanging on the cross either. We made a deal over fifteen years ago. I told you in that room in the drug treatment center, if you would believe in my Son and trust Him, I would prove to you that I am in charge. Have I not done that?" And then the tone changed to that fatherly one that I always longed for, "We need to get past your discomfort, because we have work to do here." He had given me what I needed to do the work He wanted me to do.

By the end of the day, fifty-nine teammates had ministered to over 1300 inmates in three different sessions. 338 decisions for Christ were made-- 149 of those being first time commitments to Christ. I believe that if I would not have opened myself up to that dialogue those numbers would not be the same. It's not about the numbers, but those numbers represent real people who need Christ. My initial lack of grace toward those men could have affected their eternity. What a horrible thought, to stand before God, my Savior one day and for Him to say to me, "There's somebody missing here because you decided they were not worthy of the same grace I have shown you." It is only through God's grace that I was able to minister to those men that day.

Last Fall, Forged By Fire hosted a ride out to the Ohio State Reformatory on the twentieth anniversary of the film *The Shawshank Redemption*. For me, personally, it was a day of revisiting the birthplace of what was one of the darkest, most miserable seasons of my life. We started our tour by walking through the administrative portion of the prison. I felt no particular emotion in that part of the prison, since I had never been in that part of the prison before. Walking into the chapel caused the first stirrings of emotion within me. This room was familiar. This room made it all real again.

I found myself talking and joking with people in my group to cope with the increasing sense of anxiety that I felt. I could see the entrance to the Southeast cellblocks across the room and to the left. It seemed to be almost physically pulling me toward it. I saw all of the same bars, concrete, and peeling paint. I was transported back in time to the eighteen-year-old kid who would decide to become predator in order to avoid being prey. I could still hear the cries of those who had the misfortune of being physically or mentally weak: cries that told me I would have to focus everything in me on becoming as strong as possible in every way. I felt all over again the transformation from person to inmate. From "Doug" to "inmate number 112421."

All of these thoughts flooded my mind, yet I was able to carry on as tour guide for my group. Other folks touring the prison stopped to listen to the memories of a former inmate. There are things that the brochure and audio guides can't capture. These are the things that I was able to share- the things that make it real for people. Leaving the chapel, we entered the part of OSR that was my home for a time back in the 1980s, called the East Cellblocks.

As I was sharing, a passerby was overheard by some in my group remarking to her companion, "Well, if I had been a prisoner here I certainly wouldn't be bragging about it." My wife resolved instantly not to share this with me, sensing that it might cause me undue pain. You see, my wife can be very protective of me when she feels others misunderstand or malign me. In any case, I found out about it from someone else in our group. I would like to tell that passerby that, yes, I was answering questions and even making jokes at times as I recounted prison life. Giving voice to many of these memories requires some type of comic relief just to break up the heaviness of it all. I've been told, by friends who were in our group that day, that the harsh reality of my life in prison was not lost in the humor.

Those who know me also know the outcome of the story. I openly share about my past, not to glorify wrong-doing or "doing time," but to make clear just how AWESOME Jesus Christ is. To convey any semblance of His power and grace, I HAVE to talk about the horrible state that I was in-where He found me, embraced me, and saved me from an eternity of misery without God.

Praise God that He is "no respecter of persons" (Acts 10:34, NKJV). These days, I like to tell people that there are still only two options-- not *predator or prey*-- but *with God or not with God*. That's it. The details really don't matter.

CHAPTER 17

The Academy

I mentioned that God opened *two* doors to Forged By Fire, the first being prison ministry. The other door that God opened offered another perfect opportunity to be a reflection of His grace. My wife, Tanya, is a special needs teacher working with children who have autism and intellectual disabilities. It is through her that I connected with another program in the building for youth who are at risk of failing academically, called the Academy. My wife was having a discussion with one of the Academy teachers and noticed a book laying on the table. It was about Tookey, one of the founders of the Cripps in California. I hate to ruin it for you if you're going to read the book, but Tookey went out of this world lying on the lethal injection table in San Quentin. During this discussion, the teacher said it would be nice to have a speaker who had lived a life similar to Tookey's. My wife told her about me.

Arrangements were made, and I went in and spoke to the high schoolers first. The Academy is set up so that the teachers are able to have more of a one-on-one relationship with each student in order to help them make it to graduation. It's heartbreaking to go in and see these young people making bad choices, often because of the environment that they live in. Just to give you an idea, in the last year, two students have been sent to prison, one is in the county jail right now, one is a gang member, other students are on drugs, and on and on. You know some of them, their parents are either physically not home (maybe in prison or partying somewhere) or they are at mentally and emotionally not home because of drinking or doping. Sometimes a grandmother is trying to raise them. Other students in the program come from stable homes but have other issues keeping them from being successful in school. Whatever the circumstances, *all* of the students are at a point in life where their choices have real consequences that can last for years.

Of all the things I could talk about concerning the kids, there is one topic that seems to surface in all of our conversations: Trust. Life has done things to some of them that have taken their trust away. I'm sure at some point, each of them believed it when an adult told them they were going to do something. When someone said, "Hey, I'm going to spend time with you," they expected it to happen. Unfortunately, what I have found is that these kids have been told things, and people haven't come through so often that they no longer expect anyone to honor their promises. They are not surprised when people don't come through.

There have been times when I have been sitting there with the kids when they have gotten news that a planned event wasn't going to happen. I was initially surprised to see that there wasn't much of a reaction from them. During the course of an hour-long conversation that day, I asked every one of them individually how they felt about this particular incident. The most prevalent answer was, "You get used to it after a while." I feel a great responsibility to help them understand that it's ok to have emotions. It's ok to be mad and sad. It's even ok to tell someone that you are upset with them, that you didn't appreciate something they said, did, or didn't do. The key is learning to control how those emotions are expressed.

I have personal experience with not trusting. I had the same mindset as these kids for most of my life. I know that not trusting can make you build walls to protect yourself from the pain of life. I can relate to these kids because even when I left the prison walls behind, dropped the number and picked my name back up, I was still a prisoner in my mind.

When you boil this problem down, there seems to me to be an easy fix: Do what you say you are going to do. To be fair, we all know that circumstances sometimes keep you from honoring a commitment you've made. Especially when dealing with these kids, though, I believe that these should have to be pretty important for you not to honor your word. Otherwise, you become just another on a long list of people who have let the kids down. You become part of the proof that they can't count on anybody-- that they shouldn't trust anyone. I've seen people schedule to visit these kids and then just not show up. It's true, not only did they *not* honor their commitment, they did not come back to the kids and explain the situation. People need to realize that their actions do have an impact, especially when you are dealing with kids who have already been through extraordinarily difficult circumstances.

It's not all seriousness, we do actually have fun and love on the kids when we visit. One time, we rented half a bowling alley, for example, just to bowl and eat pizza with them. It was a blessing to see the walls come down from around these kids that day, as they realized that we weren't there to lay anything heavy on them, we were just there to kick their butts bowling.

One particular activity we did with them stands out. Forged By Fire has built several relationships with businesses in the community. One of those is The Deli at Webster Street. Working in downtown Dayton for so many years and having lunch there opened the door for this relationship. It didn't take long to get to know the owners, Mark and Emily. As time went on, the conversation got around to Forged By Fire and some of the things were are involved with. We decided to partner up on something they had started the year before: making tie blankets for Dayton Children's Hospital. It had been just a family activity, but Mark, Emily, and Forged By Fire thought if we combined our resources, we could turn it into something really big. Always thinking of something to get the Academy kids involved with, I naturally thought about approaching them to ask if they would like to be involved.

I thought it would be a great opportunity for them to learn that no matter what your situation, serving others will help you put things in perspective. Somehow seeing others who are even worse off than you has a way of making your life seem not so bad. The overwhelming response was, "Yes." I think we all would agree that we can set the tone for our day by starting it out thinking about all the things we don't have, thinking of all the things that are going wrong, or thinking of all the things we do have and what is going right in our life.

The tie blankets for the sick kids in the hospital were a huge success, not only because of the number of blankets that were donated, but also because of the impact on the lives of the people who were involved. To see so many different types of people working together for this common goal at The Deli at Webster Street was inspiring. I saw my immediate family members working with my coworkers, Academy kids, men from the Fairhaven Men's Breakfast, Forged By Fire, the Blue Knights Ohio III, and The Deli at Webster Street.

For most of the first part of my life, I was involved in a lot of things that were bad. This event was especially rewarding because this time, I was the catalyst for something good. I was the common denominator among the people who participated in something positive for the community. It means so much to me to be a force for good in the world. Even more than that, though, I saw the Academy kids experience the joy that comes from doing something good for others.

CHAPTER 18

More about My Journey

While I was leading the tour at OSR, one of the men who rode up with us had heard my story as I took people through to tour the prison. During the break, he asked me, "What was *the one thing* that changed everything for you?" I instantly said, "Jesus Christ."

The Bible says that once we accept Jesus Christ into our heart, believe that Jesus died for our sins, and was raised from the dead three days later, God has not only forgiven us for our sins, but has forgotten about them too. Just because God has forgotten about some things in my life, I haven't, nor do I want to. I *choose* not to forget these things. Hopefully, so I won't repeat them and so I can use them for the kingdom. It takes a lot of practice, a lot of praying, and a lot of being led by the Holy Spirit to stand up and tell people about your past.

Sometimes, even in a group of thousands you're talking to only one person. Over my years of standing up before people, I have really worked on letting the Holy Spirit lead me in my speaking. I have been asked, "Doug, how can you go into so much detail about your life before Christ?" My reply to them is that it is very uncomfortable, but the last thing I want is for someone that's listening to think, "Yeah, he's had it pretty tough. He's been through a lot, but he hasn't been through what I've been through. I don't think there's *any* hope for me." It's very important to tell your story honestly-to not add anything to it, but also not to take anything away from it. I believe that all of us, no matter what story we have, can frame it in a way that's not crude but still has the truth in it.

When I first came to Christ, being a new creature, believing, as His Word says, that the old man has gone away, I had to be taught things. I was like a child again. That's what's so awesome about God's grace- that you can start with a clean slate. That doesn't mean that there still aren't going to be consequences for your actions before you came to Christ. For that matter, there will still be consequences for things you do *after* you become a Christ follower. God comes through on all his promises, but He plays by His own rules and that's what makes Him so awesome. You can read His Word, find out what His rules are, and trust in them. He's not going to change them on you. If you've done something that there're consequences for, you're going to have to deal with that.

As my relationship grew in Jesus Christ, and I let go of the old inside me, it made more room for Jesus. I studied His Word and learned His promises. I found the key to this whole thing: You can read the entire Bible, learn Scripture, recite it word for word-you can have it all down-and still not have the relationship I'm talking about with Jesus Christ. I'm not saying there's anything wrong with learning and memorizing Scripture, but I believe our *greatest* testimony is the life we live. It's not what we know about God, Jesus Christ, or the Holy Spirit, but our *relationship* with Him that matters. If we live our lives in such a way that people know we are a Christian without ever asking us-we know we're there. I'm not talking about perfection. I'm not perfect by any means. I'm talking about a relationship where, at the end of the day, you can bow before Jesus Christ, and say, "You know, I just didn't cut it today. I don't believe I gave you what I set out to today, but I know you're my friend. Can we try it again tomorrow?"

My knowledge of His Word grew and I started feeling the need to publicly tell people about my life. I was even encouraged to do this by the pastor of the first church I went to, yet I struggled with whether I needed to tone my personality down or not. I have been accused of being bold since I was very young, so bold that it used to get me in a lot of spots that were tough to get out of. I finally came to the conclusion that God doesn't want me to change my personality, but instead, He wants to use the boldness He gave me to glorify Him.

The way I use that boldness to glorify Him is to tell anybody who will listen about what He means to me and the miracles that He has performed in my life. As the first part of my life started to become open to people in the church, I started to hear the same thing from everybody: "People need to hear your story." To be completely honest, when this first started to happen, I thought that everyone was just being nice. As time went on, I began to talk with people who were struggling with the same things that had me in bondage before I met Jesus Christ. Seeing the same miracles in their life and knowing that God was using me and my story to make that happen, I couldn't help but want to continue in that direction.

I remember Pastor Mark telling me that he even took my story to Guatemala, and struggling with how to describe my appearance, the only thing that he could come up with to describe the prominent tattoo on my neck was "El Diablo," the devil, because of the grim reaper that is tattooed there. I figured right then that if what God has done for me is being used by other people in their ministry, that was confirmation that God wanted me to share about His transforming power myself. Scripture teaches us that the true believer will desire to share with others what God has done for them. In John 4:28-30, 39-42 (NKJV), the Bible tells us that a woman, after speaking with Jesus, then left her water pot, went her way into the city, and said to the men, "Come, see a Man who told me all things that I ever did."

I ignored the urge to share my story for so long, because I thought it was just my pride. I thought that it was part of the old me trying to get back out, the man who loved to "hold court" as my wife calls it. Sometimes when we come to Christ, we want to do away with so much of the old that we shut it *all* down, but God wants to use some of that for His Kingdom.

As rewarding as witnessing to someone was, I was soon to learn the incredible feeling of helping someone receive the gift of salvation, actually receiving Jesus Christ into their heart. The first person I led through the sinner's prayer happened to be my own father, lying in a hospital bed after they had amputated his legs. After my mom passed away, my dad's health started to get progressively worse. I knew that, short of God's intervention with a miraculous healing, my dad's life here on earth was coming to an end. As with my mother, he had beaten his body up for some sixty-five years. The last five years of his life was a whirlwind of procedures, medication, and surgeries. Knowing that the end could be close, his salvation was heavy on my heart. I remember weekly, sitting in church, watching people raising their hands and accepting Jesus Christ as their savior, and wanting desperately for one of those hands to be my father's.

Over those last five years, my father and I had put some things to bed. We could at least sit in the same room and have a civil conversation with each other. I stopped by his house after church one Sunday and got up the courage to tell him that I loved him. I really believe that he wanted to say that he loved me, but he still just didn't know how. All he could say was, "Yeah, well…" He *did* like to brag to people about his son who had given up all the things in life that had held him back and hurt him, and he even liked to tell people that I went to church. For some reason, he just couldn't say that he loved me.

As I stood there over his hospital bed, telling him about some of the things that I was involved with in the church, I'll never forget what he said. "I don't even know if I'm saved or not." I remember the calmness of Don Baughn the day I stood at the chain link fence after I got home from the treatment center, and I think he was just as excited that day about the chance to share his savior with someone as I was right then. He was just mature enough not to do anything that would embarrass someone. I remembered the words that Pastor Brooks spoke every Sunday and had everybody repeat:

1 John 1:9 If we confess our sins, He is faithful and just to forgive us our sins and to cleanse us from all unrighteousness (NKJV) and Romans 10:9 that if you confess with your mouth the Lord Jesus and believe in your heart that God has raised Him from the dead, you will be saved (NKJV).

With all that going through my mind, what I very calmly said was, "You know, we can take care of that right now." With that, at my request, we bowed our heads and I led my dad in the Sinner's Prayer.

It wasn't long before my father went to be with the Lord. His body was so ravaged with gangrene; there was just nothing that the doctors could do for him. I remember my wife Tanya and I sitting with my dad at hospice seeing the consequences of his hard life and bad choices, yet having peace in our hearts knowing that he would spend eternity with God. The last thing I ever said to him before he died was, "There's nothing left for you here. Go be with your wife," and he was gone.

Epilogue

Why I Share My Story

O ne experience I often share starts with a can of beans. Believe it or not, the best-tasting food I've ever had in my life was actually a meal I ate in prison! While in London Correctional Institution, I was locked up in Solitary Confinement, which we referred to as The Hole. To be honest, I thought of Solitary as a kind of mini-vacation from the turmoil within the prison. The cell in Solitary was always bare and could either be six by ten-foot with open bars on the front, or the same size but with a solid steel door, depending on what stage of Solitary Confinement you were in. I've been in both.

When an inmate is sent to The Hole, they strip you down, put you in a while jumpsuit and little white cloth booties, and give you a very thin mattress and a sheet, and that's it. You sit there for however many days the court has sentenced you to. It can be anywhere from three to forty-four days. I've done it all. The forty-four day trips to the hole were a little much, even for me, but the seven to ten day stays were like a vacation except for the constant feeling of hunger. You are given the same type of food as everybody else in the prison, but you get the minimum quantity. I felt hungry all the time, and Solitary was even worse because I had no access to commissary items.

Anyone can look at me and tell I like to eat; I always have. In fact, what I missed most of all was food. If you have the personality I have, you make connections in prison to get things like clothes, food, whatever you want. There are ways to get things no matter where you are in the prison. The guards don't really run the prison; they just keep you from leaving. The prisoners really run the prison. There are trustees that do a lot of the work in the prison, including in The Hole. For example, a trustee is the one who brings your meals around every day. If you know someone in general population, they can pay a trustee to deliver an item to you. A trustee can be persuaded to bring you something, even in The Hole. I had a trustee show up at my door one day with a delivery for me. It was a can with no label on it. I had no idea what was in the plain tin can, but it didn't matter. I had to get into that can! I had no can opener, but as I said, I was hungry. To this day, I still can't remember how I got the can open. By the time I got it open, though, the can was beat up, the top was jagged, and the lid peeled back just enough to see what was inside: And there they were, big red kidney beans.

I hated kidney beans as a kid! I put them into the same category as a butter bean: Big, fat, and mushy. My mom would try to disguise these beans in other meals, but I'd scrape them aside, and try not to eat any of them. Even when she made chili, I'd try to eat everything but the beans, trying not to think about how they had touched everything else. I reached in the can, scooped some beans up with my bare fingers, and took a bite. The juice dripped down my fingers, and I thought, "I've never tasted anything better." Even now, I have never had a bite as delicious as that one. I savored every bite, even as my fingers got cut up from digging in the can. The beans lit up every taste bud I had. I've had many an excellent steak, including from renowned restaurants like Frankie and Johnny's in New York City, and they weren't any better than that can of big red kidney beans in that moment.

That's the kind of hunger that we need to have for Jesus Christ! We need to experience Him and rejoice in Him with at least as much fervor as I had for those kidney beans. When we do, we will want to share that experience with others!

I truly believe that Jesus Christ did not die on the cross for us to stay on the bench. God does not want benchwarmers. He wants us engaged and involved, sharing His love with other people. One way

I do that is to talk to people about Him-to go out into the world and tell people about my life before Christ and how He has and continues to mold me. My wife and I worked together for three years to put this on paper as another way to reach people who might be struggling in their lives, maybe for the same reasons I did, maybe for reasons of their own. Although the particular obstacles people face vary, there is but one remedy: Jesus Christ. It really is possible for anyone to break free! Our prayer is that the person who is sitting and reading this book right now will believe that there is a power and authority to help them find out what the real purpose for their life is and begin walking the path that will lead them there.

God is just waiting for you to take the first step. His Word even says in James 4:8, "Draw near to God and He will draw near to you" (NKJV). It's as simple as speaking to God from the heart: "Lord Jesus, I need You. Thank You for dying on the cross for my sins. I open the door of my life and receive You as my Savior and Lord. Thank You for forgiving my sins and giving me eternal life. Take control of my life. Make me the kind of person You want me to be. In your Name. Amen."

Praying is just talking to God. Now that you've taken the first step, I highly recommend that you find a Bible-believing church and tell someone you have accepted Christ as your Lord and Savior. Find a group to plug into and a mentor to help guide you on your journey. This is not a journey to be made alone!

Bibliography

Avildsen, J. (Director). Chartoff, R., Winkler, I., and Kirkwood, G. (Producers). (1976). Rocky [DVD]. Beverly Hills, California: United Artists

Explore History & Haunting at the Ohio State Reformatory. 2014. Retrieved from http://www.mrps.org/

The Ohio Penitentiary. n.d. Retrieved June 2, 2014 from http://forgottenoh.com/Counties/Franklin/pen.html